THE SECRET OF SELECTING STOCKS FOR IMMEDIATE AND SUBSTANTIAL GAINS

BY
LARRY WILLIAMS

WINDSOR BOOKS, Brightwaters, New York

SECOND EDITION

Published by Windsor Books
P. O. Box 280
Brightwaters, N.Y., 11718

Manufactured in the United States of America

ISBN 0-930233-05-0

CAVEAT: It should be noted that all commodity trades, patterns, charts, systems, etc., discussed in this book are for illustrative purposes only and are not to be construed as specific advisory recommendations. Further note that no method of trading or investing is foolproof or without difficulty, and past performance is no guarantee of future performance. All ideas and material presented are entirely those of the author and do not necessarily reflect those of the publisher or bookseller.

THIS BOOK WAS WRITTEN FOR THOSE SPECULATORS WHO WANT TO STAND ON THEIR OWN TWO FEET AND MAKE THE MOST OF THEIR INVOLVEMENT IN THE MARKETPLACE, REALIZING THAT THERE WILL BE LOSSES AND HARD WORK ALONG THE WAY, BUT THAT PERSEVERANCE PAYS WELL.

I want to thank the many people who have increased my understanding of the market. This includes many advisory services, subscribers to my service and individuals with whom I've batted around ideas. I must also thank my staff for their patience and hard work in helping me make this book a reality. Above all, though, a special note of thanks must go to my wife and my parents. My good fortune in the world would never have happened without them.

LARRY R. WILLIAMS

TABLE OF CONTENTS

Page

PREFACE

Writing an author's update for a book that was written 15 years ago is a real challenge!

The real challenge is that I am tempted to change some of what appeared in the original copy of this book. But in reading and rereading the book I see that the book simply does not need to be reauthored or rechanged.

The tools, techniques, indicators and strategies discussed in the book are as valid now as they were in 1969 when the book was written.

There are two things that I would like to stress upon people reading *The Secrets of Selecting Stocks,* for the first time.

First, is that these indicators have stood the test of time.

I have received letters and phone calls from people who literally swear by the accumulation/distribution technique discussed in this book. Perhaps the greatest thrill of writing this book came in the form of a postcard sent to me from a lawyer who was on vacation in the South Pacific. The postcard simply said, "Larry, my wife and I are taking this vacation because of the profits we made following the indicators and especially your accumulation/distribution technique as you presented it in your book. We both are enjoying the sunshine and thank you very much."

Much of the technical work you see being done today by leading advisors is a spinoff of what appeared in this book, so for no other reason than historical purposes I do not want to change what was originally written about in the book. This book seems to have been a Genesis for a great deal of thinking about technical approaches to the market.

The indicators still work and they still work in the same fashion. As they say, if it is not broken why fix it?

Perhaps the longest term value to come from the book is the major forecast made in the book under the 39 year pattern that I believe I have been able to isolate that has called some of the very important major turns.

Notice that in the 15 years since the book was written there have been many doomsday calls for economic disasters, stock market crashes, and all sorts of arguments from the purveyors of pessimism about how bad the world is going to get. In fact, what has taken place has pretty much been in line with the forecast made in this book.

A study of this major forecast will give you an economic road map of where the economy and stock market is headed for a long time to come.

Yes, there will be a major crash in the stock market. The big question is not that it will occur, but when it will occur. The answer to that is in this book.

My own trading style appears to have smoothed pretty much in gear with what I see most traders doing. We cut our teeth trading stock and then moved into commodities. Most of my own trading experience is now in commodities because commodities are more easily traded, especially due to the low discount rate in stocks. Interestingly enough however, the tools that I use to trade commodities with are very similar if not the exact same tools discussed in this book.

The markets have been my life. It has been a good one, I hope it is for you as well.

Cordially,

Larry Williams

CHAPTER ONE

MY MILLION DOLLAR STOCK MARKET CONCEPT

MY MILLION DOLLAR STOCK MARKET CONCEPT

A cold wind was blowing through Wall Street in the Fall of 1971. After a dramatic 100 point rally ignited by President Nixon's announcement of Wage & Price Controls, the market suddenly reversed itself and began to plummet. Things looked bad. The DJIA had just broken its support point and fallen to a new low. Many analysts announced that we had begun a Bear market.

I didn't think so. That was because a few of the select indicators I keep were giving bullish readings for the stock market. Reflecting back upon it, I'm certain I was as influenced emotionally by the break to new lows as anyone. Things looked dismal. I felt a knot in the pit of my stomach. But when I turned to look at my indicators, the ones I will be discussing in just a few more chapters, I noticed they were in a distinct bullish area. Their message was clear: they were telling us to buy stocks. So I did.

SELECTING STOCKS TO OUT PERFORM THE MARKET

Within just a very few days, the market began one of the strongest advances it had made for many years. Shortly before the market began its tremendous 22% up-move from the 800 area to the 960 area, I bought four stocks for my own account.

The four stocks I purchased showed a net increase of over 52% in value during the next six months, whereas the popular averages increased only 22%. Had one purchased and held the same amount of these four stocks as I purchased at the November low point, he would have had a profit of slightly over $308,000.00 some 5½ months later.

I am giving you these facts to show why I believe my stock selection is of value and to substantiate some of the things I am going to be discussing with you.

With a little bit of luck in calling important market turning points, one should be able to buy stocks that show about the same percentage moves as the DJIA. However, when you consider the four stocks I selected for my own portfolio showed a gain almost three times greater than the Dow, it does appear there is predictive value to the system.

1

I could go beyond what happened in my own personal account. You see, at that time I was also writing a stock market letter and, of course, made specific recommendations with our buy signals sent out during the first part of November, and again, just a few days before the low point was reached.

The stocks we were recommending at that time were Federal National Mortgage at 75 and AMF at 38. Levitz we recommended in the 80 area, North American Mortgage at 35, MacDonald's at 61, Pickwick at 37, Syntex at 66, Burroughs at 131, and IBM at 292. On the 16th of November, we also advised purchasing Lennar Corp at 45, Ponderosa Systems at 57, American Research & Development at 44, Walt Disney at 104, and Polaroid at 90. As you can tell from the number of recommendations we made at this time we were indeed quite bullish on the market.

Exactly five months later, this uniquely selected portfolio showed a sizeable gain. Ponderosa Systems, which had split two for one, was selling on an adjusted basis at 118, up 61 points. Syntex was selling for 115, up 49 points, American Research & Development was selling for 70, up 26 points, Disney for 165 up 61 points, Polaroid for 132, up 42 points. Federal National Mortgage, which had run up as high as 108 on an adjusted basis for a stock split, was selling at 97, up 21 points on the adjusted basis. AMF was selling at 66, up 28 points. Levitz, which had run up as high as 162, was selling at 135, up 55 points. North American Mortgage was selling for 34, down 1 point, MacDonalds at 102, up 41 points, Pickwick for 48, up 11 points, Burroughs for 175, up 44 points; International Business Machines for 395, up an incredible 103 points. The only stock to show a sizable loss was Lennar Corp. which was then selling at 36 down 9 points. The initial portfolio value was $115.5 per share. Five and a half months later the value was $168.8. The portfolio had increased 46.1%. Keep in mind that this was during a period of time when the market itself, as measured by any of the popular averages, was up about 20%. Our specially selected stocks performed twice as well as the averages.

I believe this is conclusive evidence that my stock selection system, the one you are about to learn, does have the unique ability to select stocks that are going to out-perform the market on both the long and short sides. What happened in my account, the $308,000.00 profit I mentioned earlier, was not a random event due to luck or my good looks. It was due to my stock selection system that has been proven time and time again to have significant forecasting value.

Making money in the stock market is far from simple. Don't let the above few paragraphs lull you into feeling Wall Street is an easy path to instant riches. It isn't . . . just like anything of value, it takes hard concerted work to be successful. But let me also point out that I have been able to consistently make money trading stocks in my own account as well as in public recommendations in the advisory service I used to publish, "Williams Reports."

WHY THE WORD FORECASTING IS IMPORTANT — My abilities to usually call market turns and individual stocks is the direct result of a good deal of study and research into the marketplace. In the beginning, I tried to latch on to other peoples' supposedly successful methods.

When it comes to making money in the market, I'm not proud . . . I'll try any halfway logical method or system to generate profitable trades. That means I've read all the books on fundamentals, methods and technical systems. In fact, I even dabbled a bit in some interesting research on stock market and astrological relationships.

It wasn't long before I learned that if a system is to be profitable it must forecast what will happen in the future.

That little sentence is the real key to understanding the stock market. If an index or approach is to work, it is because it has forecasting ability. In examining various market theories, my first thought is to study the basics of the system to see if the raw data has forecasting significance. If not, the method cannot work! Along the road to the discovery of my key to the stock market, I tried and studied many, many different approaches. I'd like to share a few of my views on the more common systems for stock market trading and investing in an effort to help you separate the wheat from the chaff.

WHAT I LEARNED ABOUT CHARTS

At some point in his life, every market participant, be he trader or investor, takes a look at charts and reads a few books on how to chart your way to wealth. I found the only people charting their way to wealth were the authors of the books! Try for the life of me, I could not find a workable charting program, formation, or whatever other mysterious forecasting element was supposed to exist on the charts.

In today's mail I received a flyer from one of the widely followed chart services. Their central advertising claim is that charts could help traders and investors because, as they said, "Charts are a natural for stock trading, since they give the full results of all supply/demand factors. They reflect insider buying and selling, "smart money" accumulation and distribution, important news before it is published — in fact, everything that anybody knows or does."

This is the general view of those entrenched in the chartists' camp. They feel charts, through various formations and configurations, reflect the true supply/demand picture and thus have forecasting value. There are many books on charting and almost as many chart formations or patterns as there are stocks. But, by and large, most chartists look for a few basic chart patterns.

Chart 1

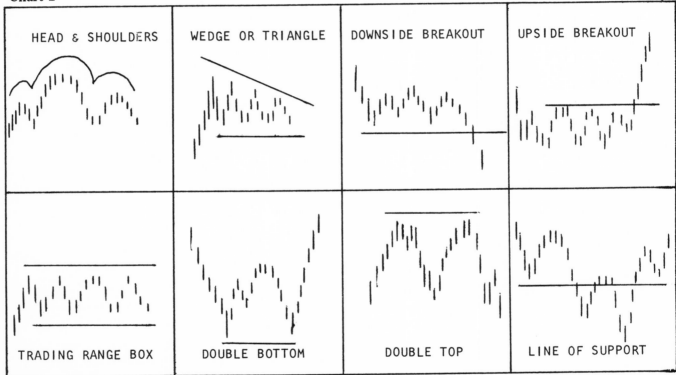

Chart one shows several of the more basic chart formations such as the head and shoulders, boxes, diamonds and a pennant. You will find these patterns illustrated in any of the books on stock market charting.

Keep in mind that charting is based on the assumption that a chart correctly depicts the supply/demand battle. As such, charts enable one to spot developments that depict a bullish or bearish supply/demand pattern. Supposedly, these patterns repeat and forecast future market or stock action. It's certainly a nice concept.

But two things bother me about the frayed-cuff chartists . . . First of all, I do not know of any chartists who are really very wealthy or doing exceptionally well in the market. To quote economist Paul Samuelson, "They all have holes in their shoes." Seriously, of the thousands of people I know in the market, I cannot show you one chartist who is making money!

More importantly, when I notice charts of other activity, such as rainfall in New York City, traffic deaths in Los Angeles, or the reproduction rate of Canadian Lynx, those same darned supply/demand patterns show up on the charts!

This is incredible . . . when charting series of numbers that have no relationship to supply/demand (certainly we cannot argue there is a supply/demand relationship to the number of deaths in L.A. County) the same head and shoulders, wings, wedges and upper case Outer Mongolian breakouts occur.

The continual re-occurence of the same "supply/demand" patterns in non-supply/demand phenomena must splash a good deal of cold water on any forecasting validity the chartists might try to conjure.

I suppose the validity of charts will be discussed for many years to come. There will even be some lucky chartist who attributes his luck to charts and writes a book or market letter about his charting system. But, as long as the same patterns appear in rainfall statistics and traffic death records, I'm going to have to remain a non-believer. You are urged to do likewise.

WHAT I LEARNED ABOUT MOVING AVERAGES

One of my attempts to make a killing in the market centered around the use of moving averages. Several authors and market letter writers had turned me on to the standard use of moving averages. I thought I'd give their methods a try.

A moving average is simply an average of a series of numbers. The only difference is that the average changes each day as we add the new day's information and subtract the data or information for the number of days ago for which we are running the average. Thus, in a 20 day average we add up all values for the last 20 days and divide by 20. To make this a "moving average" we wait until tomorrow's close, add that figure to our sum and subtract the figure from 21 days ago and divide by twenty.

As with any mathematical average, the resulting values represent a smoothing of the raw data. Take a look at the chart shown here and you can get a better feel and understanding for moving averages than I can tell you in thousands of words.

Chart 2

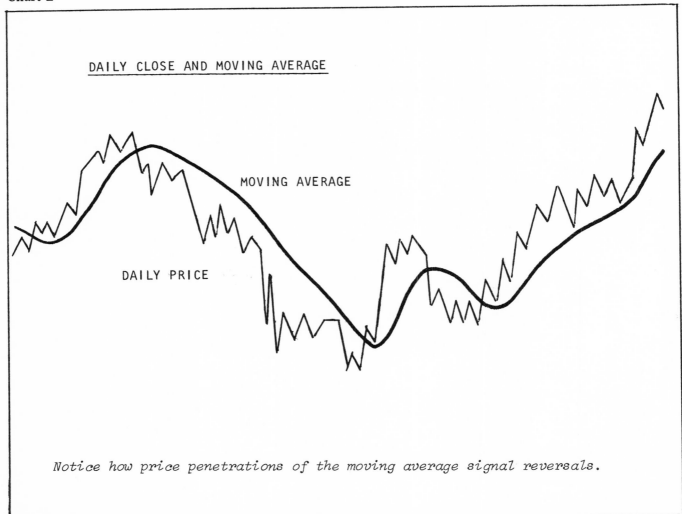

DAILY CLOSE AND MOVING AVERAGE

MOVING AVERAGE

DAILY PRICE

Notice how price penetrations of the moving average signal reversals.

One thing you'll quickly notice is that a moving average acts as a trend line or band of resistance and support to the raw data. Also, when the raw data rises above the moving average, it continues moving up. When the raw data falls below the moving average, the up trend has been reversed and the raw data moves sharply lower.

The usual moving average methods are based on penetrations of the moving average. Thus, if a stock's price rises above its **10** week moving average, a buy signal is given and when it falls below a **10** week moving average, a sell signal is produced. On paper, and with some stocks, the method appears absolutely phenomenal.

Funny thing though, try as I might I couldn't make any money using the moving average system. I was perplexed. I re-read the rules, but again, I lost money. Finally a bolt of lightening hit me ... the moving average method worked great when it worked ... but when it didn't work, Oh Brother!

What's more, promoters of the moving average methods selected stocks for which their system worked best in the past. They did not bother to show stocks the method did not work on. Nor did they bother to carry their system into the future. What they did do was find a stock or two that had a big up move and a big down move. Their moving averages were placed on this trend and captured a large part of both moves. Stocks that did not have large moves but traded in narrow confines were not shown because these situations produced losses!

Most of the moving average systems are based upon a 10 week average. The big question is, as always, will the moving average system work and if so to what degree?

Recently articles have appeared in the Financial Analyst's Journal discussing various longer term moving averages. One study randomly selected 30 NYSE issues between 1960 and 1966 and tested 100, 150, and 200 day moving averages. Signals were generated by either an absolute penetration of the moving average or a percentage greater than the moving average — a filter — above and below the average itself.

Using the 100 day average with no filter produced a 57% loss of capital. Using a 200 day moving average produced a drop of 34% in starting capital. Whether one used a 100, 150 or 200 day moving average with no filter, or a 2%, 5%, 10% or 15% filter, he would have lost money during this 6 year period!

In June 1969, in an effort to devise a profitable trading method, I ran a test of 10 stocks for 450 market days using shorter term moving averages of 3, 4, 5, 7 and 10 day durations with filters of —3%, —1%, +1% and +3%.

With the benefit of hindsight and the use of what was at that time the world's largest computer, I was still not able to devise a profitable trading strategy based upon the moving average method!

THREE NEW WAYS TO USE MOVING AVERAGES — If moving average systems are of little value, as the above statistical research demonstrates, is there still some way they can be used? I think so.

To my way of thinking, there are three good ways to use moving averages. The first method is to simply observe the trend of the moving average and as long as the trend of the moving average is up, assume the stock will go higher. When the trend of the moving average is down, assume the stock will go lower. In other words, trade the long side of a stock only when the moving average is up and trade the short side only when the trend of the moving average is down.

Another way to use the moving average draws upon the penetration of moving average by price itself. At first glance this seems contradictory because I've just shown that such penetrations do not produce very reliable signals.

What I'm suggesting is that you act upon signals from moving average penetrations if, and only if, other technical or fundamental criteria have been met. In other words, once you are certain a stock is bullish or bearish because of another factor, you can then act on signals from the moving averages. In short, you need to weed out the bad moving average signals. This is done by developing a set of criteria that must first be met before you will act upon any moving average signal. In fact, the moving average signal is the final indication to take action as it simply announces that the trend has been reversed.

A third way to use a moving average involves using it to measure a stock's momentum or cyclical harmonics. This is a more involved topic and will be discussed in detail later on.

WHAT I LEARNED ABOUT FUNDAMENTALS

It stands to reason that if a company's fundamental position is one of great bullishness, the stock price will stage a handsome advance. The only problem here is identifying what fundamentals are bullish, or bearish, for that particular company, industry and market situation at the time. Or, so it seems.

Some of the most powerful fundamental situations have never advanced or declined while some of the most fundamentally bearish stocks doubled and trippled in value!

Several years ago, there was a hot little number on Wall Street called Four Seasons. Fundamentally the stock was a short sale and many knew it. But the fundamentals did not prevent the stock zooming from 20 to over 100! About two years after the big run up, the fundamentals caught up with the company and they filed for bankruptcy. But in the meantime, the fundamentalists that shorted the stock in the $20, $30, $50, $60 and $70 area were clobbered and they too "filed" for bankruptcy.

General Motors is another good case to study. The long term outlook for GM can't be too bad. Yet GM made its all time high in 1965 and has never participated in any substantial up move since then. Time and time again you'll see many fundamentally bullish stocks take nosedives while the fundamentally bearish stocks fly to the moon!

HOW TO TELL IF A STOCK IS FUNDAMENTALLY SOUND — In all of my research I have found only two reliable measures of fundamental value. One concerns itself with yields, the other with the company's growth rate.

CHECK THE YIELD — The first and most important fundamental statistic is the stock's yield. Generally speaking, a low yield is bearish for a stock and a high yield is bullish. But just what is a low yield for any given stock? This is best obtained by checking the stock's historical 10-20 year record. Almost without exception, you'll quickly see that all major tops in the stock come at a time of low yields and usually this low yield will be about the same at all tops.

By the same token, all the stock's important lows will usually be found when the stock is at a high yield and always about the same general level. Thus we can establish overvalued and undervalued levels of yield for each stock based upon that stock's historical record.

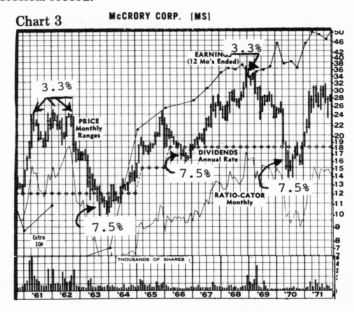

Chart 3 shows one such example. Notice how all the tops come at low yields of just about the same valuation.

And the bottoms? It's just the reverse, all the bottoms come at a time of high yields and all the bottoms are marked by the same general level of undervaluation and high yield.

Short sale selections should come from stocks showing very low historical yields. Long candidates come from the high yielding stocks.

Remember, the high or low yield for one stock, say IBM, will not be the high or low yield for another stock, say G.M. It's all relative to each stock's individual historical record.

9

HOW TO DETERMINE A COMPANY'S GROWTH RATE — There are a good many ways to look at a company's fundamental growth. The most typical are the P/E ratios. Another method seeks to establish the company's growth rate while others look at net sales. All are, to some degree, helpful but usually do not give us adequate figures to compare one stock with another.

The payout time formula solves this.

This simple formula is nothing more than the number of years it will take earnings per share, compounded at the firm's current growth rate, to reach the price of the stock. Let's say the earning per share is $1.50, the growth rate is 20% per year, and the current price is $30.00. It will take about 16 years for the compounded earnings to equal the stock's current market value.

Lets's take another stock with earnings per share of $1.00, a growth rate of 15% and current market price of $3 a share. In terms of the annualized growth, this does not appear to be as good a buy. But its payout is only some 9 years! It represents a better buy. The lower this payout figure is, the better a fundamental buy you have located.

HOW I DISCOVERED THE MILLION DOLLAR CONCEPT

As you can tell, I've spent a good deal of money and effort on research trying to crack the market's mystique. One thing that always fluttered around the back of my mind while I looked at charts, moving averages, point and figure charts, and fundamentals was this: all these things do not, in and of themselves, make prices move up or down.

No matter how bullish the technical structure of a stock is or how impressive its rate of growth and yield figure, these things do not and cannot be guaranteed to influence prices!

Then it hit me . . . the only thing that can possibly make a stock go higher is an imbalance of buyers and sellers. It is as simple as that. When there are more buyers than sellers, prices will advance. Conversely, when there are more sellers than buyers, prices will go down . . . regardless of the fundamentals!

As simple as the concept sounds it took several years of research to arrive at a meaningful way to break down the relationships of buyers and sellers as well as methods to identify the difference between professional and amateur buying.

Realizing it was the imbalance of buyers and sellers that influenced prices, I began studying the various groups of people in the market, such as the odd lotters, specialists, floor traders, etc.

Through this process, I discovered a reliable method that breaks down each day's buying and selling activity in any stock into the approximate number of shares bought and sold that day. This method, actually a precise formula, tells me at the end of each day about how many shares were on the buy side and how many shares were on the sell side. From these figures, I can begin analyzing the supply/demand battle.

I also discovered there is one certain chart pattern that indicates if a stock is under professional accmulation or distribution. This is a very simple pattern and has nothing to do with traditionally known chart formations. The comparative pattern graphically tells us what stocks have been under heavy buying and are in strong hands as well as the stocks that have been undergoing professional selling and are in weak hands.

A 13 POINT GAIN JUST LAST WEEK — Let me first tell you that my two phase method for anlayzing accumulation and distribution is not infallible. It has made few errors, but, by and large, the method has worked wonders for me.

Just last week McDonalds Corp, the hamburger people, appeared to be under heavy accumulation in my work despite a sharp market break. My figures said the stock was ready for an upmove. I put in my order for 1,000 shares at 49¾. All measures of accumulation were impressively bullish despite the soft market. This stock had been priced for an upmove.

As I write this, 7 market days later, MCD is selling at 62, up over 13 points from my buying indications which came at the 49-50 range. My million dollar, two part concept, is based upon the central tenent that stock prices advance if, and only if, there are more buyers than sellers and decline if and only if there are more sellers· than buyers.

We analyze the buying/selling syndrome in two statistically valid ways to detect professional accumulation and distribution. The exact formulas and patterns will be given to you in a moment, but first you must understand the importance of the supply/demand bearing on forecasting stock prices.

11

CHAPTER TWO

MY FIRST TOOL FOR SELECTING THE BEST STOCKS

THE TWO METHODS I USE TO IDENTIFY ACCUMULATION & DISTRIBUTION

As I've said, the only thing that will push the price of a stock higher is a preponderance of buyers. Conversely, the only thing that will drive prices down is a preponderance of sellers.

My study into the accumulation/distribution area was prompted by an old timer's casual remark in a board room. At the time, I was trying to figure out what tape reading was all about. I spent just about every market hour watching prices chatter by on the ticker. I wasn't making much progress and certainly wasn't finding it possible to "read" the tape.

This particular board room was frequented by a somewhat daffy old gal who was always going to buy or sell stock, but never did. She must have missed the boat by just a day, or a point, on hundreds and hundreds of big winners. At least that's what she claimed, and I'm inclined to believe her. It was unfortunate.

One day, a stock she had been following, widely touted as being a super strong stock, began to fall. In a matter of minutes it was down three points. By the end of the day it was off five dollars. The next day gave the lady no relief as the stock continued to fall despite the fact the market was rallying!

The pressures of losing were getting to her, and she said out loud, to no one in particular, "Why in the hell is that stock going down?"

My old timer friend, sitting in the back row, loudly said that he knew exactly why this hot number was going down!

Well, that was just too much for the little lady to take. She scurried back to the fellow, demanding he tell her exactly why the stock had been plummeting. It was obvious she was upset that the fellow hadn't told her sooner. However, her anger was tempered by the fact that someone finally was going to give her the secret to her stock's activity.

The old timer, I'll call him Don, had been a broker for many years. He lived through the crash (many brokers didn't), and in the process had acquired a great deal of insight into people and the market. Of those of us in the board room he was the only one with substantial amounts of money, making him the resident guru.

Don could contain himself no longer. He leaned far, far back in his chair and bellowed out, "Any fool can tell you why your stock has been going down . . . there've been more sellers than buyers!"

Everyone roared! Old Don had "taken in" another trader. The gal didn't think it was funny though, and insisted she be told how to know when there are more sellers than buyers. For that Don had no answer.

The episode I've just described was one of the turning points in my career. For years I had tried many, many stock selection and timing systems. But upon reflection, I saw that none of them attempted to break down and identify the amount of buying or selling taking place in the market. They were all based on something else . . . something that might effect stock prices from time to time, but the special forecasting ingredients were not always present.

Don had hit the nail on the head! Indeed, stocks move due to an imbalance of buyers and sellers. All I needed to do was develop a method to measure these components. I'm not going to bore you with the myriad of techniques I fooled around with before I finally arrived at what I feel are the two best ways of identifying professional accumulation and distribution. My very first studies revealed that there are many types of buyers and sellers in the marketplace, but that only a few, a group I've labeled "the professionals", were worth following.

DISCOVERING THE PROFESSIONALS

There's an age old question in the market that would give ample thought for the greatest of all the masters of Zen Budhism. Usually these monks meditate upon probing, seemingly unanswerable questions. But imagine giving them the market's most difficult question, "For every buyer there is a seller. Therefore, how can prices change as buying and selling is always equal?" I'm no Zen monk, and believe me it was confusing to ponder upon this unique supply/demand relationship. My research eliminated much of this confusion as I soon discovered that the one for one relationship has little bearing on prices. Instead, I learned it is more important to notice at what time and price buyers are willing to move into or out of a stock. That's part of the secret!

A specific example may help. In the Spring of 1971, I recommended Bausch & Lomb in my advisory service when the stock appeared to be under accumulation in the $50 area. In the service we rode it up to $150, for a 100 pt. gain! Then in the 150-180 area, additional buying came into the stock; but this was not professional buying, it was uninformed buying. We knew this because the stock already had doubled in value! Professionals, the really smart people, were buying in the $30 to $60 range. Those were the people who took the largest gains — the smartest investors.

13

We also shorted Bausch & Lomb at 180-190 and had the pleasure of seeing it topple, slamming down to the 60 level. The same situation held true on the downside. People buying the stock in the 180 area were the uninformed, the last to get aboard, if you will.

The point I'm trying to get across is that in analyzing the buy sell relationship, you must take two things into consideration. They are:

1. WHERE THE STOCK HAS BEEN
2. WHERE THE STOCK CAN GO

Another important thing to notice about buying or selling is what is taking place in the market itself. Those investors or traders aggressively accumulating stock on days the market is down are indeed courageous in their views. The normal reaction to a down day is to stop buying. This is best seen in volume trends. As the market moves lower, daily volume continues to diminish.

So, when we spot buying taking place in spite of a down market, we have a sign that someone knows what he's doing, and we're going to want to follow this type of informed trader as much as we can.

COMPARATIVE STRENGTH, THE SECRET TO FOLLOWING ALL STOCKS

Many people have been amazed that I can follow just about all stocks traded and in an instant tell if the stock has been under basic accumulation or distribution. There's really nothing to it other than an understanding of the preceding paragraph.

You see, to spot professional accumulation, all we need to do is find an example of steady and determined buying in the face of a weak stock market. When this happens we have a good idea that professional buying is taking place.

Professional selling will show up when we see consistent and determined selling in the face of a strong market. That is, when the market is surging up, but selling pressures enter a particular stock we can bet that we have a stock undergoing professional, informed selling.

The effect of buying and selling is easiest to see in the price trends of individual stocks. You will be shown other ways to fine-tune and fully analyze accumulation and distribution, but it's imperative for you to remember that the effects of buying and selling will first be exhibited in the prices themselves.

THERE'S A PATTERN TO EVERYTHING — ESPECIALLY ACCUMULATION

Realizing the first visible signs of accumulation or distribution appear in a stock's price puts us far ahead of the pack. Now we can begin to concentrate on identifying accumulation and distribution in terms of patterns with the aid of simple stock charts.

As the many followers of my service know, I'm not particularly "big" on chart formations and traditional chart signals. In fact, it's my opinion for the most part, chartists "know not what they do." But that doesn't rule out the intelligent use of charts.

HOW TO USE STOCK CHARTS

Remember, we want to detect professional accumulation and distribution. We've established that the best way to do this is to find individual stocks whose price action differs from the overall market. This can be done easily by taking a chart of any of the popular averages, Dow Jones Industrial, NYSE Composite or the Standard & Poor's and simply comparing the market average configurations to any individual stock's price trends.

In an instant you can analyze virtually any stock by comparing its action to the action of all stocks, as represented by a broad market average!

To further simplify this evaluation technique, I've devised what I call the accumulation and distribution patterns. All you have to do is take note of the market average and the action of any stock to see if the accumulation pattern is present. If so, you have a potential candidate for a buy. If the distribution pattern is present, you have a potential short sale.

THE ACCUMULATION PATTERN

To detect accumulation, we look for bullish divergence between the market itself and the stock we are attempting to analyze. Bullish divergence can best be seen when a stock fails to be as severely affected by selling pressures as the broad market. Another way of putting this is that a stock exhibits accumulation when it does not match the market's downward moves. Instead, the stock holds up better than the averages on market down moves and rallies stronger on market rallies.

This is quickly discernable on chart 4. You can see from our example of Telex in the summer of 1969. Notice that the Dow Jones Industrial Average repeatedly declined to new lows, stair stepping down and down and down.

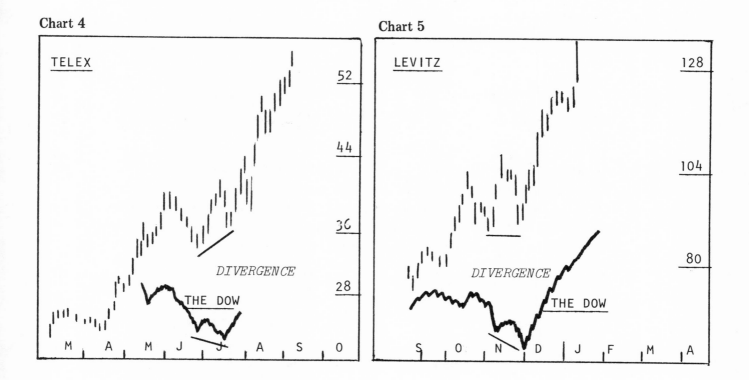

Chart 4

Chart 5

However TC not only failed to move to progressively lower prices, it actually held above its intermediate term lows while the market fell below its corresponding points. This is a sign of extremely strong accumulation! Study it well.

In spite of a very weak market, the holders of this stock did not panic. They held onto their stock even though the market was taking a clobbering. Thus, we can assume these people had special knowledge. Severe weakness did not disturb their positions for they knew higher prices were on the way.

Additionally, new buyers were willing to come in and hold up the existing price structure. In short, while most all other stocks were declining, someone, somewhere, had bullish convictions strong enough to step in and buy this stock regardless of overall market conditions.

What more could we want? Current holders of the stock simply refused to sell, while flurrys of weakness were quickly met with additional buying. As they say, the stock was in strong hands. It was under professional accumulation.

Another good example of the accumulation pattern can be seen in chart 5 of Levitz Furniture as compared to the Dow Jones Industrial Average. Notice again we see the market falling to new lows. But this time, instead of seeing the individual stock price merely hold its own, as with TC, Levitz not only held its own, but kept moving up making higher highs and higher lows on each successive stock market move.

Let's analyze the situation once more. While the market was moving to new lows, the Bears could not force the price of Levitz down. Why? That's an important question.

Referring back to what I mentioned earlier, remember that a stock moves up only if there are more buyers than sellers. What was the situation with Levitz? Were there more buyers than sellers? Obviously, yes. Were these strong or weak buyers? Very strong! After all, on just small market rallies, (which were actually only reactions in a general downtrend) Levitz was able to zoom to new highs.

SOME POINTERS

I use daily charts to compare stocks with the market. There is no need to keep the charts yourself. There are scads of chart services and I'm listing the ones I like at the end of this chapter. All you need to do is get a clear sheet of tracing paper and make a tracing of the market average and then overlay this with the stock's price average. You then have an excellent comparative basis with which to begin your analysis.

The greater the divergence between the market and your stock, the larger move you should expect the stock to make once it begins. I guess what I'm really saying here is that divergence of a few days will forecast moves of a few days duration. Divergence of a few weeks will forecast moves of a few weeks and divergence of a month or more will forecast extended, long lasting moves.

It is particularly important that you compare your stock with the market at critical junctures. (By this, I mean important market reversal points.) The fact your stock has held up better since last Thursday is not as significant as the fact the stock has held up and performed much better since the last important top and bottom.

THE DISTRIBUTION PATTERN

In case you haven't guessed it, the distribution pattern is just the reverse of our accumulation pattern. What we're looking for here is a stock that has consistently underperformed the market. The most apparent example would be a stock that has failed to rally to a new high while the market has moved to a new rally high.

Chart 6

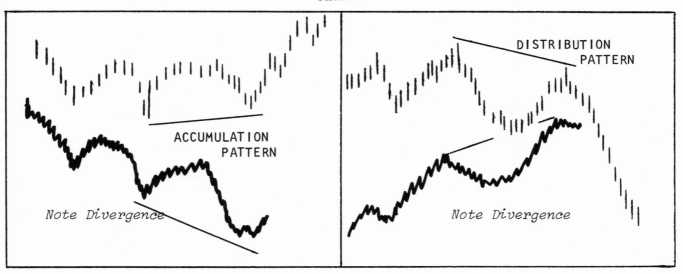

As you study chart 6, notice that while most all stocks, as represented by the averages, were able to appreciate in value, this particular stock was not. Selling was coming in at a time of overall market bullishness. Certainly we could not ask for better signs of professional selling or distribution!

So, in a classic distribution pattern we will see the market move up to a new rally high, while a stock under professional distribution will fail to make the same new high. The extent to which it falls below this new high gives us an indication of how agressive the distribution is. The greater the failure, the more hurried the professionals are to get out of the stock.

There are other ramifications to this selling pattern. Let's take a look at a few. I'd like to begin by showing you the Spring 1970 chart of Atlantic Richfield. We did not have a classic pattern here. The classic pattern will not always be present. Nonetheless, ample signs of distribution can be discovered.

In the case of ARC, we see the market staged a dynamic rally from A to B. This rally was strong enough to lift the averages, i.e. most stocks, back above their previous lows at point C.

But how about ARC? What happened here was a far different story. True, the stock rallied along with the market, and as there was no new rally high in the market, we did not have the classic selling pattern. But, notice how feeble the rally was, especially in reference to the previous low point at C . . . the same low point most all other stocks were able to rally above. Did ARC follow suit? No, it didn't even come close to getting back to this same price area. It was under professional distribution!

Chart 7

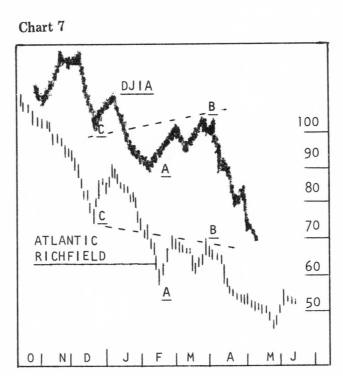

A different version of this distribution pattern can be seen in the chart of Natomas, another great trading vehicle. All we need do is compare the overall stock market rally from A to B with NOM's rally from A to B at the same time. Which displayed the greatest strength? The market. What did that tell us about NOM? Simply that it was under distribution. While the averages rallied, NOM barely held its own, managing only to "rally" in terms of a flat line, while most other stocks were rallying at a much sharper angle.

Obtain a copy of any old Trendline chart book, a few sheets of tracing paper and see for yourself how effective this simple method is in detecting accumulation and distribution . . . separating the men from the boys so to speak.

Chart 8

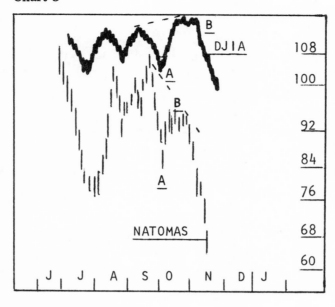

HOW TO BEST USE THE PATTERNS

Making money in the market involves the use of a combination of stock selection and market timing. You can begin working right now on the first part — stock selection — by scanning all the issues you trade or all the issues in the chart books you have, to pre-screen and select the strong and weak stocks. It takes about ½ hour to scan the total universe of all stocks listed in the all-inclusive chart books. Those of you who have your own charts, will be able to quickly ferret out those under accumulation and distribution.

This is a real boon . . . a major breakthrough, in stock selection, for it enables you to focus your attention almost instantaneously on stocks that show promise! There's no need to try to seek out every hot story and tip you hear. Nor need you spend countless hours pondering over financial statements. What's more, if you do hear an interesting story about a stock you can check it out, confirm or invalidate it in just a matter of minutes by checking directly the stock's action in the marketplace, seeing for yourself if it shows the broad, overall signs of accumulation or distribution. Do the hard facts of professional action justify the story? The answer is there in black and white in the chartbook!

The patterns I've just unveiled should be your broad, overall selective method. After scanning many stocks you can narrow your attention to those few showing the most bullish or bearish patterns and then begin to follow these issues closely.

20

ADDITIONAL POINTERS

As I said earlier, the longer lasting the bullish or bearish divergence, the more significant for longer term moves. Because of this, the method can be of real value at what you feel may be major stock market tops or bottoms.

Indeed, one of the best long term selection methods is simply this: spot the stocks that have not fallen to new market lows as the market enters into those hard-hitting selling climaxes that snuff out the life in the Bears and ignite the spark of the next Bull market.

A further refinement of this same technique uses it to compare the various group averages, such as the Chemicals, Mobil Homes, Coppers, etc., against the broad market averages to spot the groups of stocks showing the strongest accumulation or distribution. Then narrow down your investigative work into those two or three select groups showing the pattern you are looking for. By doing this you can pre-screen all groups in about 15 minutes, virtually covering all stocks listed on the Exchange. That's faster, and a darn sight cheaper, than any computer system yet designed! Fortunately, most all weekly chart services include charts of the various groups. In the event you do not want to follow a chart service, the back page of BARRON'S contains 36 groups and gives the weekly closing price, net change, etc., so you can chart your own group indices.

In screening stocks you will find several that fit the overall signs of professional accumulation or distribution. You'll then need to select one or two from this group for your account. This further screening is done by selecting the ones that show the largest price and time divergences with the market. Remember, check both price and time divergences.

Frequently, I find myself "forcing" a stock to fit the accumulation or distribution pattern. Every time I've done this it has cost me money. Do not try to read something into your stocks that isn't there. Nor should you leave out or disregard the bearish implications because of a pre-disposed bullish disposition.

<table>
<tr><td>Trendline
354 Hudson St.
New York, N.Y.</td><td>Wall Street's Top 50
Box 14096
Denver, Colorado 80214</td><td>3 Trend Security Charts
208 Newbury St.
Boston, Massachusetts 02116</td></tr>
<tr><td>Comparative Market Indicators
Box 1552
Bellevue, Washington</td><td>Mansfield Stock Service
26 Journal Square
Jersey City, N.J.</td><td></td></tr>
</table>

CHAPTER THREE

MY SECOND TOOL FOR SELECTING STOCKS

MY SECOND TOOL FOR SELECTING STOCKS

The newcomer to the stock market would be amazed and perplexed by the amount of research fellow market buffs conduct in their spare time. I did, and still do, my share of research into new indicators, trading strategies etc. The overwhelming part of my research has produced nothing but failures and false starts.

Fortunately, a few gems have percolated through the reams of paper, computer printouts and squiggly charts I've drawn late at night. One such gem is the formula I use to measure the amount of accumulation and distribution taking place in any stock, at any time and any place.

For several years I toyed around with what market technicians call On Balance Volume, a technique originally written about in great detail by two fellows, Woods & Vignolia, in the mid '40's. Their work was popularized by prolific Joe Granville in his interesting book, "A NEW KEY TO STOCK MARKET PROFITS." The essence of either method is that one constructs a flow line of daily volume for a stock by starting at any base number, say 5,000, and adding all of today's volume, say 500 shares, to the base line if the stock is up for the day, thus giving a new reading or base figure of 5,500.

Should the stock be up the next day, that volume is added to the new figure of 5,500. Thus, if the stock was up on 1,000 shares, the new number would be 6,500 (5,500 + 1,000). Should the stock run into selling pressures the following day and decline on 800 shares, you would subtract the volume giving you a new figure for the day of 5,700 (6,500 − 800). One continues constructing this flow line updating it each day, keeping a running or cummulative figure.

I liked the central thesis behind this approach, but found the activities of the market place left much to be desired. There were several ways of interpreting the figures, and frequently bad . . . even disastrous . . . . . . signals were given.

The basic approach — that of making some sort of flow line of the amount of buying and selling taking place in a stock — stuck with me. By trying to improve upon this basic tenet, I eventually stumbled across my almost perfect formula for accurately measuring accumulation and distribution.

As with most really good ideas, luck played a large part in my stumbling upon the secret ingredient! I had been playing around with an idea that saw all traders as being at war with each other — the buyers and the sellers. The results of their war-like efforts could be measured each day by the amount of net change for the stock. An improvement here was to look beyond the stock's net change and view the entire range for the day.

Chart 9 shows a true picture of stock action. We start to see the beginning of a very important relationship. The relationship is simply this: One can tell how the daily battle has been going by noting where the stock closes for the day compared to where it has been. If a stock has a high for the day of 62 and a low of 58, we have reference points to compare with the closing price. If the stock closes at 59, it is quite clear that a good deal of selling forced the stock down from its high.

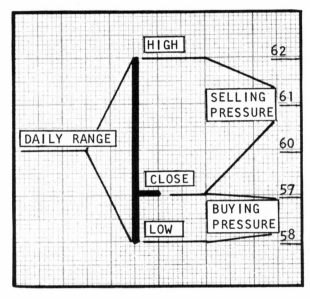

Chart 9

In fact, even if the stock closed higher today than yesterday, but nonetheless closed very close to, or at, its low for the day we would have to conclude that not all the volume for the day was on the buy side. A good deal of it was selling!

For many months I batted this idea around, then one morning it hit me! I usually arrive in my office 10-15 minutes before the opening. That's 7 am West Coast time, and it's usually a good time to think. The phone hasn't started ringing yet, no one else is in my office so I can watch what happens. This particular day I wanted to closely follow the daily volume action of one of my favorite trading stocks, Natomas.

Shortly after the opening, I saw a funny thing happen to NOM. The stock opened down ¾ of a point below yesterday's close on a block of 1,500 shares. From there, trading began and when the final bell rang, NOM had managed to trade some 44,500 shares and closed unchanged for the day, exactly where it was the previous day.

At first glance one would say Natomas showed no net change for the day . . . that buying and selling pressures were equal. But how about that upmove from where it opened on a mere 1,500 shares to where it closed up ¾ of a point. What was that?

HOW YOU CAN TRACK THE DAILY SUPPLY/DEMAND BATTLE

It is possible and quite feasible for you to closely track the true supply/demand battle anyplace in the world where you have access to a quote machine, stock broker or The Wall Street Journal once you grasp the importance of what I've just written. That's because the professionals give clear cut signals of what they are doing if you will only take the time to follow them on a daily basis.

Making money in the stock market is not easy . . . it is hard work. Our goals of immediate and substantial gains are quite high. Such goals can be reached, but only if you will pay close attention to what you are doing. This does not mean you have to spend all your time watching the market, but you do need to carefully review daily stock market figures.

TRACKING THE DAILY SUPPLY/DEMAND BATTLE IS ALL-IMPORTANT

So that you fully comprehend the importance of the daily supply demand battle, I want to shed some further light on how stocks trade. I want you to have a thorough understanding of just what happens each and every market day and give you a feel for the battle on the floor of the Exchange.

To do that I watch price action on a daily basis to see what the professionals are doing . . . to see who is winning the perpetual demand/supply battle. I do this in a most unique way. In the next chapter I'll give examples of the exact mechanics of the method, but for now I just want to impart the basics and give you a better understanding of how to identify professional buying and selling.

LET'S SHATTER SOME PRECONCEIVED NOTIONS

The mere fact that a stock is up, or down, for the day implies in no way whatsoever that it has been under more accumulation or distribution. Price changes from yesterday to today do not reflect what is really taking place in the stock.

That's a pretty strong statement! When you ask your broker for a quote, he'll give you the price and then say it's up or down x points for the day. If it's up for the day you conclude there've been more buyers, if down, more sellers. That is not so! If you are to succeed in the market you must shake that preconceived notion out of your head.

You see, there's a battle, I mean a real battle, every day on the floor of the Exchange between buyers and sellers in each stock. Perhaps these encounters explain why most stock market people are so antagonistic!

The battle between buyers and sellers ends each day with the final bell. Someone has won that round. The next day it's a new battle, but at the end of each day we can sit back and see who was the winner.

It's good to know the battlefield and what its parameters are. The battle begins every morning when a stock first opens to trade. Usually, within the first 15 minutes, all stocks are opened for sale. A value point has been established, the gloves are touched and the battle is on.

If the Bulls initially get command, they will start forcing the price up. The contrary, of course, will occur if the Bears gain control of things. This means the daily high for the stock is established by the Bulls. The distance from the morning's opening to the daily high shows the power of the Bulls.

The Bears show their daily power by driving prices down. Hence, the distance from the morning's opening to the low point represents their pressures, or the amount of selling. The bearish forces are measured as the price range from the opening to the low. The bullish effect is the measure from the opening to the high.

There's another figure we have to work with. That's where the stock closes for the day. The easiest way to use this figure is simply to see if the closing price of the stock is higher or lower than the morning's opening price.

If the stock opens at $56 and closes at $54, we can say the Bears won the day's battle. After all is said and done, prices declined from the opening level. Had the $56 opening seen a 56¼ close (or any amount greater than $56) we would say the Bulls captured the upper hand.

There's a third alternative. If the stock closes for the day at the same price it opened, we then have a stalemate day wherein neither the Bulls nor the Bears were able to gain control.

Years of research have taught me that almost always the opening price is due to inexperienced traders throwing in "buy at the market, on the open" orders. These people are, so to speak, the sacrificial lambs who cheerfully enable the specialist to set the opening price. These orders are not professional. What's more, stocks almost always open on very, very light volume. An actively traded stock that usually trades 35,000 shares or more per day may open up on only 2 or 3 hundred shares. Any price change from yesterday's close to this morning's opening is highly arbitrary and not to be trusted.

NOW WE KNOW WHO WON THE BATTLE, BUT BY HOW MUCH?

As you can see, it is possible to tell who's winning the battle, but we need to weigh the victories and losses. Here's why: Let's say we have one day where the buyers win and one day where the sellers win. That information alone leaves us at a stalemate. We cannot say who is really ahead.

ENTER VOLUME

But all is not lost for we can further define the winner of the daily battle by breaking down the daily action into percentages. This is done by determining what percent of the daily action the Bulls most likely controlled and what percent the Bears most likely influenced. When all factors are equal, we will have a 50% buy, 50% sell ratio.

If the Bulls are substantial victors, we may see a 60% buy and a 40% sell day. In the next chapter you will be given my exact formula to arrive at these figures. Right now we're just working with the concept. Just take for granted that it is possible to construct a percentage figure for all stocks that will reflect the approximate buying and selling action during the day.

This gives us another dimension. In our example we can further evaluate this by comparing the percentage of buying on both days. Let's say the percent of buying on the buy day was 80% buy and 20% sell. The next day, the sell day, sees a 60% sell day and 40% buy day. Knowing this we can then tentatively identify that during these two days the buyers were in control, as our buying percentages were 80% + 40% totalling 120%. Our selling percentages were 20% +60%, for a total of 80%. Buyers were in command over the two day period.

But even this may not be enough. That's why we compare the percent of buying or selling with the stock's daily volume. Volume represents the true figure, the raw data, of accumulation and distribution.

Thus, in an 80% buy day, we take 80% of the day's volume as buying volume or accumulation. In a 20% buy day, we take 20% of the volume as buying volume and have an accurate reflection of the amount of buying and selling taking place in any stock, any time. Nifty huh?

While my friend Don and the little old lady are still sitting in a brokerage office trying to tell if there are more buyers or sellers, ending up more confused than ever, we are able to tell exactly what percent of today's volume is most likely buying volume and what percent is selling volume! We have conquered the supply/demand question by identifying its elements and breaking them down into a workable structure!

HOW TO TELL WHEN THE PROFESSIONALS ARE IN CONTROL OF A STOCK

Professional traders are a pretty nice group of people. They tend to be less emotional than the average trader, more calculating and less eager to rush into a stock or market move. They have enough funds that they can take their time, sit back and see what is happening.

This is one of the reasons that real professionals seldom, if ever, buy stocks on the opening for the day. They wait, letting other people establish where the stock will begin trading. After that point has been determined, the professional trader, and specialist, can then make a judgment. At the opening price, is the stock over or under valued?

If the stock appears overvalued, they will begin selling the stock, conversely if it appears undervalued, they will begin buying the stock. In either event, what happens after the opening is (A) largely determined by professional traders and therefore (B) a reflection of professional activity.

If you want to see what the professionals are doing in your stock, watch what happens from where the stock opens to where it closed. The specialists do this, as do the few professional traders, but the public just wants to know if the stock is up or down for the day.

Let's not discount the role of the specialist in this little game. He can pretty much arbitrarily set the opening price for the stock. Thus, if he thinks the stock is going higher, it's no problem to open the stock down a point or more on a scant 500 to 1,000 shares. He and his buddies then load up on "cheap stock", and begin to move the price up. This little maneuver enables them to buy stock at something like a special discount sale held for the professional traders!

Time and time again I have seen stocks open up anywhere from ½ to 3 points from the previous close on less than 1,000 shares . . . then big blocks come in and new moves begin. Perhaps this is why so few specialists ever go broke in the market and why seats on the New York Stock Exchange are so expensive!

In summary then, to detect what the professionals are doing to your stock watch what happens from the opening to the close. If the stock closes above its opening, they are buyers. If the stock closes below its opening, then they were sellers for the day. I make both of these statements unequivocal of where the stock closed today in relationship to yesterday's close.

MORE EXAMPLES FOR YOUR BENEFIT

The picture seen in chart10reflects the net change for the day as measured by the distance from one day's close to the next, just as most people keep charts. Directly underneath this traditional line of price action, I'm showing a line constructed by taking the amount of price change from the opening to the close. The line moves up if the close is higher than the open, down if lower.

You'll quickly see that this is an almost X-Ray technique that enables us to see when the professionals are exiting or entering the stocks while simple price action itself looks deceptively bullish or bearish. Notice how this line leads stock prices!

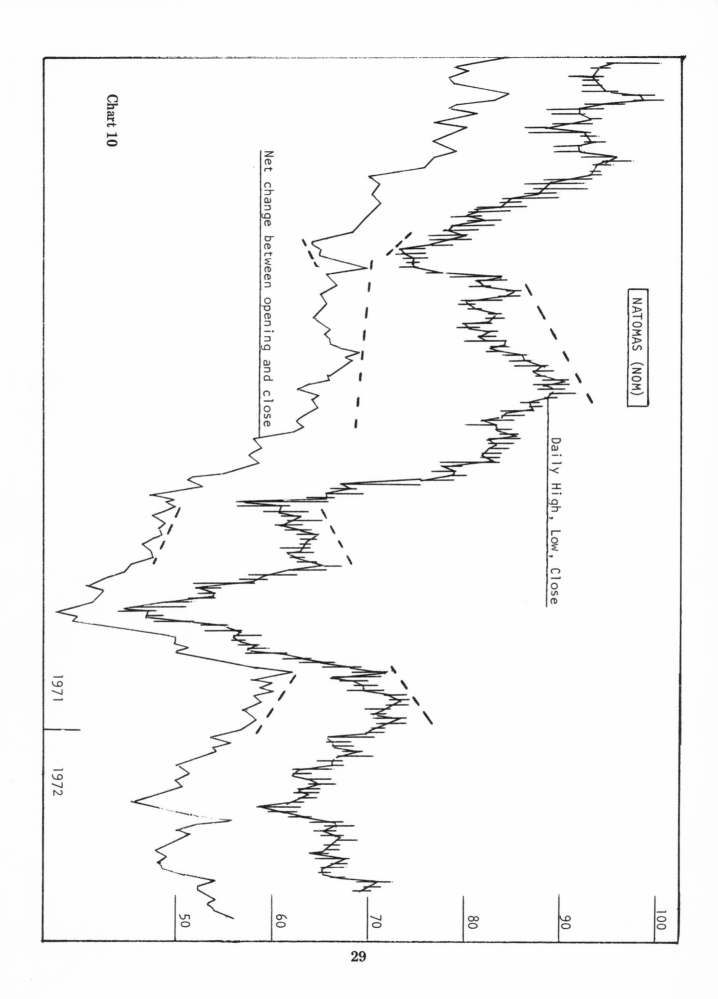

Chart 10

NATOMAS (NOM)

Net change between opening and close

Daily High, Low, Close

CHAPTER 4

HOW TO PROFIT FROM THE ACCUMULATION DISTRIBUTION FORMULA

PUBLISHER'S NOTE:

In order to perform some of the calculations in this book, the daily opening stock prices are needed. While not published in the major business newspapers at this time, these prices are readily available. A number of computer services provide this information. Your broker would also have access to this information.

So you can either use a computer service, contact your broker, or alter the equation slightly (as described below).

If the opening prices are not readily available to you, Mr. Williams has advised us that a still valid representation of the daily supply/demand battle can be constructed by substituting yesterday's close in place of the open in the formula.

This substitution will also give the same degree of accuracy and excellence in timing and selection. The amount of accumulation is determined by taking the distance from the previous close to today's high. This is one unit of buying.

Next take the distance from today's low to today's close, the other unit of buying. Add these two units together and you have the total buying figure for today. The total selling figure is arrived at by taking the distance from yesterday's close to today's low and today's high to today's close.

Add the total buying figure and total selling figure. Then, divide this total figure by the buying figure and you have the percent of buying for the day.

If yesterday's close is higher than today's high the first buying unit is zero. By the same token, if yesterday's close is lower than today's low that selling unit is also zero.

HOW TO PROFIT FROM THE ACCUMULATION DISTRIBUTION FORMULA

Up to this point, you have learned about the importance of price patterns and how certain signs of accumulation can be seen when a stock holds up better than the market. Signs of distribution are seen when the stock does not hold up as well as the market.

You've also learned about the importance of professional activity and the vital need to watch what happens from the opening to the close. Now it's time for you to learn how to tell how much of the day's volume was buying or selling volume.

But before we proceed, let me again stress the importance of the chart pattern formations mentioned in chapter two. I have the feeling that a lot of readers will skim over that chapter finding it a bit simplistic for their sophisticated minds. Believe me . . . those patterns are as important a signal of accumulation and distribution as the actual formula I'm going into in this chapter. Do not underestimate the value of looking at stocks versus the market to prescreen those under basic accumulation or distribution.

By doing this, you narrow down your universe or field of vision to just a handful of stocks, thereby avoiding anything but the strongest issues. You can then begin looking at the accumulation work being done by the professionals, in terms of volume, to select the strongest stock or two from this already dynamic list of vehicles.

HERE IT IS . . . THE MILLION DOLLAR FORMULA

The formula I finally arrived at to measure professional accumulation and distribution is calculated by finding the difference between the stock's high and low for the day. We then find the difference between the close and the open. We now have two numbers, one telling us the total daily range, the other showing us the net change from the opening to the close.

The next step is to divide the close-to-open distance by the high-to-low distance. This resulting figure is the percentage of net buying or selling for the day.

The third and final step is to multiply today's volume by the figure just obtained. Our resulting answer (the net daily accumulation/distribution figure) shows how much volume was buying or selling volume for the day. This net daily A/D figure is then added or subtracted to a cummulative A/D flow line just as with traditional On Balance Volume or the more familiar advance/decline line. More on that in just a few minutes.

In a concise form the equation is this: Close minus the opening, divided by high minus the low, times daily volume = net buying or selling volume for the day (net daily A/D figure). This is equated as $\frac{Close - Open}{High - Low}$ X total volume = net buying or selling pressure for the day.

If the opening price is lower than the close, your net volume figure for the day will be positive or a buying figure. This number is added to the daily A/D line. If the close is below the opening, it is a negative number showing more selling volume. The figure is subtracted from the previous day's A/D line.

WHY DO WE USE VOLUME?

It is possible to use just the price difference between the opening and close to get a feel for the amount of accumulation taking place in a stock. However, only volume moves stock prices and frequently, as the realities of the market place show, volume gives signals of an impending move as it represents what big professional money is doing. By tracking volume we can visually see what the mutual funds, specialists and large investors are doing with their money.

This is important. As an example, if a stock is up ½ point from its opening two days in a row, it's hard to tell which of these days saw the most accumulation. But if we know it was up on **5,000** shares one day and **10,000** shares the next day, it's an entirely different story. We then know which day saw the most accumulation despite the fact the price move was equal on both days.

HOW TO CONSTRUCT A FLOW LINE OF PROFESSIONAL ACTIVITY

Now that we've been able to arrive at a pretty accurate reflection of the daily buying and selling pressures we need to know how to use these figures and then learn how to read them for their crystal clear buy and sell signals.

Earlier you were told how a traditional On Balance Volume line is constructed. That is the same process I use to take advantage of the insight of my accumulation work. In other words, when I first "work up" a stock, I arbitrarily choose a base number, say 5,000 and then begin adding the net daily accumulation or distribution volume figure as dictated from the above formula to this base figure.

This means on days when there is more buying the net daily A/D figure is added. On days of more selling the net daily A/D figure is subtracted. That's all there is to this concept. No more math! It's so simple some people have trouble. They want to run moving averages, expotentials or some other figure. I think my research into these figures has covered just about all aspects of the numbers and the mathematical approaches! I found the simplest was the best! Remember, the accumulation flow line is constructed by just adding or subtracting today's net daily A/D figure, as arrived at by the formula, to yesterday's figure.

Perhaps an example will clear up any confusion that may exist. I'm showing below six days of trading activity for BAUSCH & LOMB. The figures are pretty much self-explanatory except the final figure . . . the A/D line column which represents the impact of today's net daily A/D figure to the previous day's A/D line figure.

Please note that I round off all eights into decimals carrying them to just one place. Thus, 34 1/8 = 34.1, 34 1/4 = 34.2, 34 3/8 = 34.3, 34 1/2 = 34.5, 34 5/8 = 34.6, 34 3/4 = 34.7, 34 7/8 = 34.8 and 35.00 - 35.0. It is much easier to convert to decimals and work in tenths than it is to work in eights. The above conversion table is easy to memorize.

Also, I drop the last two digits of the daily volume figure, just as most newspapers do. Hence the volume shown for the first day of 564 actually represents 56,400 shares. I have found it is easier to work with the smaller number, and the results are identical.

				VOL-	CLOSE	HIGH	*% X	NET DAILY	A/D
OPEN	HIGH	LOW	CLOSE	UME	—OPEN	—LOW	VOL =	A/D	LINE
35.2	36.5	34.7	35.8	564	+ .6	1.8	.33	+186	3208
36.2	38.2	36.1	37.6	789	+1.4	2.1	.66	+520	3728
38.3	38.5	37.5	37.7	414	— .6	1.0	.60	—248	3480
37.3	38.5	37.0	38.0	277	+ .7	1.5	.46	+127	3607
38.0	30.0	37.8	38.8	425	+ .8	1.2	.66	+280	3887
39.7	39.8	38.2	39.0	949	— .7	1.6	.43	—408	3479

*Close minus open, divided by high minus low, equals the net % of buying or selling for the day. Next, multiply the net % times daily volume to obtain the net daily A/D figure.

Readers not steeped in a mathematical background, myself included, may want to carefully review the figures to see how the final answer was determined and how the A/D line flows in response to the daily volume times the % of buying or selling.

I keep a loose leaf notebook with my stock pages in it. Each sheet is ruled off to give me a column for the open, high, low and close, volume and accumulation line. You do not need to have a column for the % of buying or selling if you use an adding machine. You can leave this figure in the machine then hit the multiplication button and put in today's volume. Then add or subtract this net daily A/D figure into the previous days A/D flow line figure.

SOME TIME SAVING TIPS

1. If the stock's opening and closing prices are the same, buying and selling were equal and you need not do the equation. Simply carry forward yesterday's A/D line figure.

2. If the opening price is the same as the daily high, and the closing price the same as the daily low, all of the volume was selling volume. Thus, you need not run the formula. Just subtract the day's total volume from the previous A/D line figure.

3. If the opening price and the daily low are the same and the close and the high are the same, all volume was buying volume. Again you need not run the full formula. Just add the day's total volume to the previous day's A/D line figure.

At first glance the above formula may seem complicated or time consuming. Let me assure you that it is not the case. It takes about 30 seconds per stock, per day, to post these invaluable figures. Admittedly, it takes some time to understand the formula, but in a little bit of time you'll be able to quickly see what is happening. Then the figures will almost "run themselves". Really!

HOW TO SPOT THE BASIC BUY SIGNAL

My records show that superb buying opportunities present themselves when a certain condition develops in the trading pattern of the stock's price and volume as represented in the A/D flow line. Simply put, this pattern is one that sees the stocks falling to a new low while at the same time this new low in price is not matched by a new low in the A/D line.

The majority of the time the price action will be the same as the A/D action. It is only when they diverge from each other that we can glean forecasting information from the data. I view the price action as largely an artificial attempt by influential money to cause people to do the wrong thing at the right time. Thus, price frequently falls apart, the stock has apparently collapsed. That's the impression given from studying just the price structure.

However, when we examine the volume structure we get an x-ray view of what has been taking place in terms of real money and in terms of accumulation and distribution. We can then see whether an apparent collapse in price is justified and warranted in light of the volume action.

WHAT THIS MEANS

When the price decline has not been matched by a similar decline in the A/D line, we are onto something. This pattern, a new price low not confirmed by a new A/D low, tells us the price collapse was most likely artificial and an attempt to draw the sellers out of the woodwork and sell their stock to the professionals. Reasoning a bit further we learn that if the professionals are willing to manipulate prices lower at the same time they are buying, they obviously have their sights set on higher prices.

WHAT THE BASIC BUY SIGNAL LOOKS LIKE

On the insert here I'm showing what I refer to as the classic, basic buy signal given by the accumulation/distribution figures. As you can see, the price of the stock fell to a lower low than where it was last supported. On the surface this looks negative.

However, on checking the A/D line, we see that this price weakness was not equalled or confirmed by the professional buying and selling. In fact, the A/D line stayed impressively higher and above its previous comparable low point. Indeed, the pros supported and bought the stock on the decline. Thus, we can assume they have greater things in store for the price structure over the next few days, weeks or months.

Chart 11

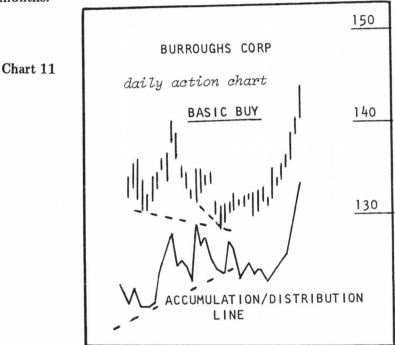

HOW TO IDENTIFY THE STRONGEST POSSIBLE BUY SIGNALS

Another feature of this method is that it enables you to visually select the strongest signals. Let's say you have isolated two stocks as potential buy candidates. Both show better price action than the market and both show accumulation has entered them. Then compare the two to arrive at the stock under the strongest accumulation. This is done by simply noticing the difference between the divergence of the two stocks you have selected. What stock shows the greatest divergence between its price action and its A/D line pattern? Find that stock! It is the best of the two candidates.

Chart 12

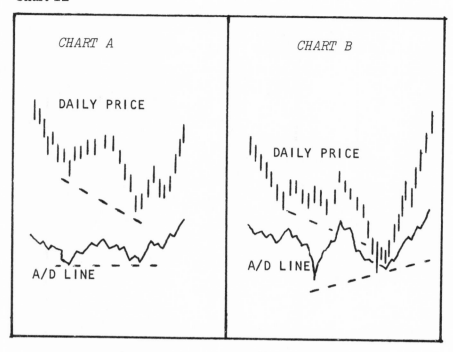

The examples given here should give you an even better feel or indication of what to look for. Notice how stock A clearly fits all our buying criteria, but its A/D line has falllen a bit further than stock B.

Incidentally, sometimes you'll see stocks suffer large declines in price while the A/D line barely, if ever, dips. This happened in Disney right at the start of an 80 point move. I also recall it happening in Polaroid. The stock had been trading in a wide swinging trading range. But . . . its A/D line was shooting skyward telling us the stock would break out of the trading range on the upside and steam ahead. Indeed it did, from the low 80's to the 140 area!

HOW TO SPOT THE BASIC SELL SIGNAL

The basic sell signal is just the reverse of the basic buy signal! That makes things simple. What we're looking for here is a stock that has rallied to new highs while the A/D line refrained from confirming the new high in the price structure. When that happens, something has got to give. It is almost always the price structure itself.

You see, prices are maintained or held up by the underpinnings of volume. If the underpinnings are weak and crumbling, the price structure will soon come tumbling down until volume and price are once more back in gear.

36

Chart 13

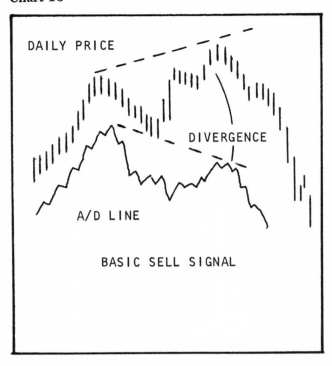

DAILY PRICE

DIVERGENCE

A/D LINE

BASIC SELL SIGNAL

WHAT THE SELL SIGNAL MEANS

The sell signal means that professionals are distributing the stock, applying heavy selling pressures to it, despite the apparent rise in price. This is a very bearish omen as it forewarns the pros are bailing out. If they no longer want the stock . . . neither do I!

The actual selling pattern you are looking for is illustrated here. In this example we see the price rallying to a new short term high. Is this a valid up move? How do we know? We know by checking the A/D line to see what it says about the rally.

In this particular case, we see the A/D line did not rally to a new high. In fact, it fell to a new low. Conclusion? The stock is under aggressive professional distribution. It is going lower.

HOW TO IDENTIFY THE STRONGEST POSSIBLE SELL SIGNALS

This part of the A/D line study is like the section on spotting the strongest buy signal. What you should be looking for is what stock shows the greatest divergence between its price action and its A/D. Look for the stock that has a splendid new high in price while its A/D line has literally fallen out of bed. That is the stock you want to sell or sell short.

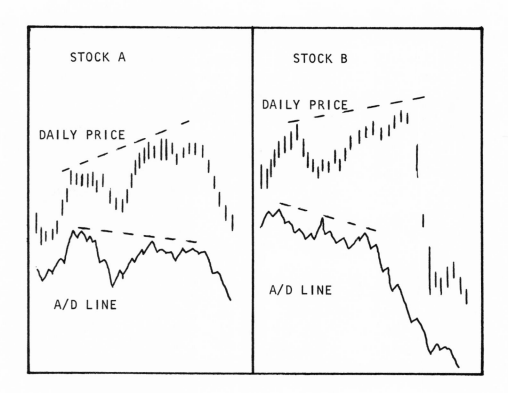

Some examples should help. Notice here how stock A has rallied to a new high along with stock B. Price structure alone does not tell us which stock is the best selling candidate. So what do we do? You guessed it . . . we take a peek at the A/D line to see which stock has been under the most distribution.

In this case, it's pretty easy to tell the difference. Stock A has had some rally attempts in the A/D figures. But look at stock B. What a disaster . . . the A/D line has fallen constantly despite the price rally. Incidentally, these are not hypothetical examples, but right out of my personal chart book.

THE IMMEDIATE PROFIT SIGNAL

From time to time I have made immediate profits by noticing a special formation in my A/D line work. I'd like to share it with you. This immediate profit signal has nothing to do with the buying or selling patterns and formations so forget those for just a minute.

The immediate profit signal occurs in just one way. It is not frequent, but when it does come look out, a rapid price move is on its way!

The signal involves a comparison of the price action and a certain occurrence in the A/D line. The price action I look for is what you know as basing or consolidation. The chart shown here gives several examples of what we can call basing or small trading areas. The price moves back and forth for several days or weeks. It is locked in the narrow confines of buyers and sellers fighting each other off at the top and bottom perimeters of price evaluation.

While this price pattern is developing, we suddenly notice a tremendous surge in the A/D line from one day's data. That is the tip-off and your signal to get in and buy the stock.

The one day massive accumulation figure will shoot the A/D line skyward, breaking substantially above the trading range pattern the A/D line has also been in. It tells us the big boys can wait no longer. They have finally begun their move and the move will be to the upside. Buy it!

You can make a pretty good living just waiting for these jumps to occur in the A/D line work. I admonish you not to confuse the A/D line jumps with total volume jumps. That is not what we are looking for. We want to find large and extraordinary increases in the A/D line itself, while the price remains in the confines of the trading range.

The direction of the A/D line jump forecasts — in advance — in which direction price will come zooming out of the trading range corral.

THE CHINESE

Chinese philosophy and concepts can teach us much about ourselves and the market. Later on I want to discuss the tremendous value of their Yin and Yang concept. But for now, I'll just refer to their great adage that one picture is worth a thousand words and proceed to give you actual examples of the basic buy and sell signal plus the immediate profit signal.

I've made notes right on the charts and have attempted to do my best to show you what things I look for. Don't skim over these pictures lightly. Study them if you wish to profit from this book. Notice the subtle nuances between the stocks and their A/D line. I have purposely not marked all the A/D signals. Why don't you start looking now for the basic buy and sell signals. That's exactly how I began!

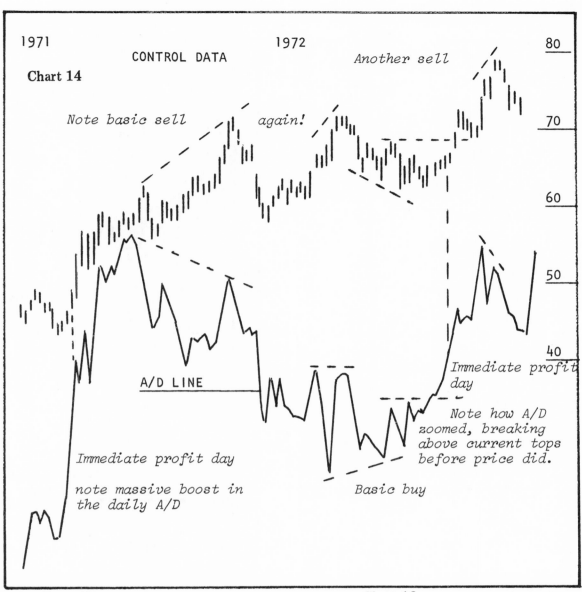

1971   1972   80

CONTROL DATA

Chart 14

Another sell

Note basic sell   *again!*

70

60

50

A/D LINE

40

Immediate profit day

Immediate profit day

Note how A/D zoomed, breaking above current tops before price did.

note massive boost in the daily A/D

Basic buy

Chart 15

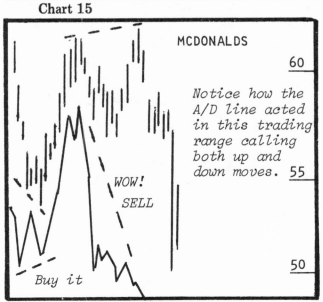

MCDONALDS

60

Notice how the A/D line acted in this trading range calling both up and down moves. 55

WOW!

SELL

50

Buy it

Chart 16

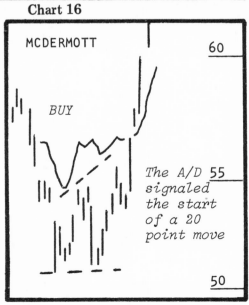

MCDERMOTT

60

BUY

The A/D 55 *signaled the start of a 20 point move*

50

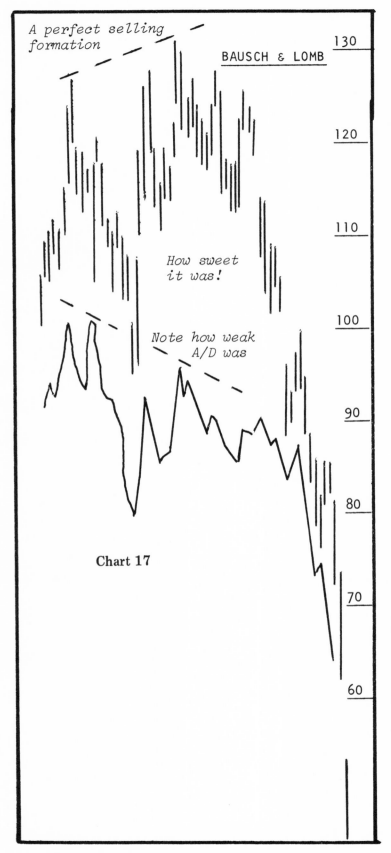

Chart 17

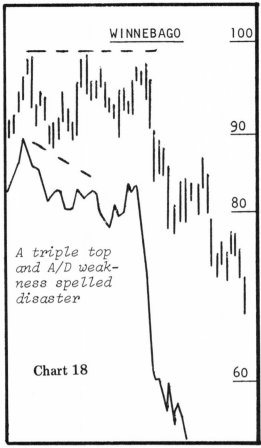

Chart 18

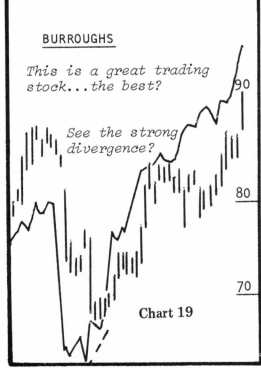

Chart 19

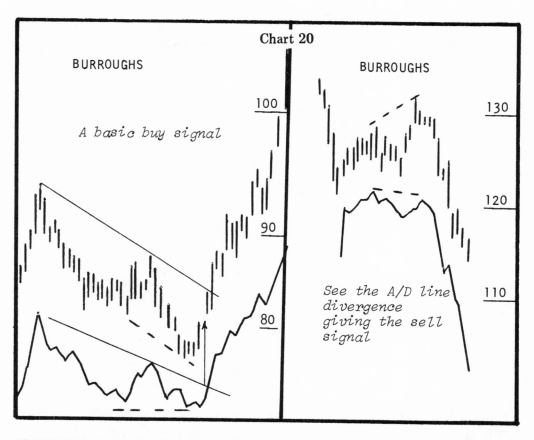

Chart 20

BURROUGHS

BURROUGHS

A basic buy signal

100

90

80

130

120

110

See the A/D line divergence giving the sell signal

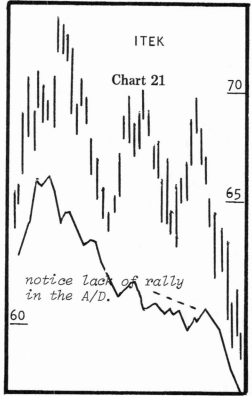

ITEK

Chart 21

70

65

notice lack of rally in the A/D.

60

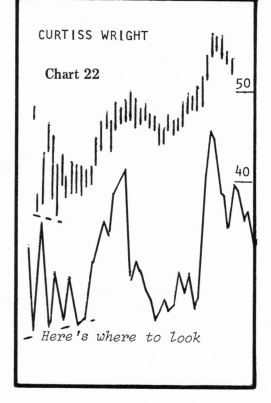

CURTISS WRIGHT

Chart 22

50

40

— Here's where to look

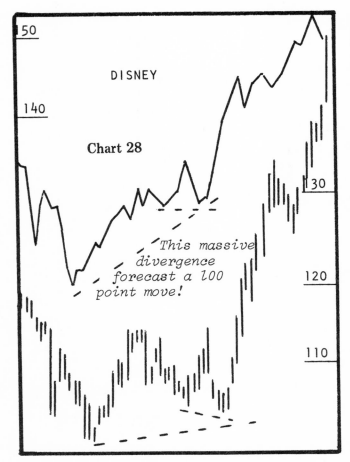

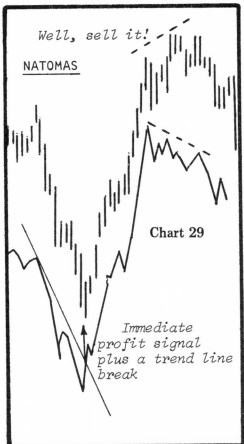

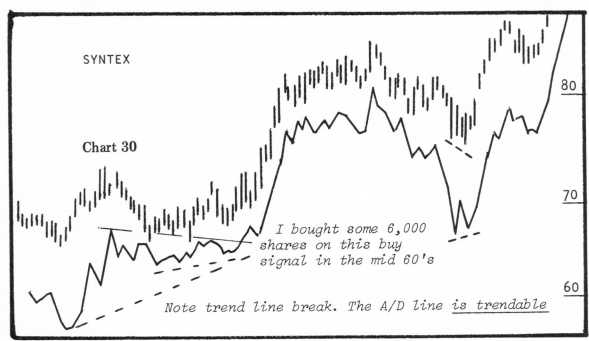

CHAPTER 5

SHOULD YOU FOLLOW THE SHORT

OR INTERMEDIATE TERM TRENDS

AND HOW TO DO IT

SHOULD YOU FOLLOW THE SHORT OR INTERMEDIATE TERM TRENDS AND HOW TO DO IT

Selecting the right stock is about 50% of the battle. The rest is a matter of selecting the right time to buy the stock. The two decisions we have to make as traders or investors are what stock to buy and when.

I've seen hundreds of market participants and have found that they have precious little knowledge of what type of investor they are or what they are trying to get out of the stock market.

One minute they are traders, the next minute long term investors. One of their biggest problems is that they continually change their self image as well as their goals. It's no wonder they fail.

If you are to profit in the market you must know who you are and what you want.

This point was clearly driven home to me in the brokearage firm I used to visit. One of the chaps in the board room was a pretty well-to-do doctor who was going to do all he could to educate me about the market. He began by telling about his latest purchase. I don't recall the stock, but I'll never forget the good doctor's glowing remarks about the company. Earnings had been up 5 years in a row. They had a better product, better sales, better financing, etc.

In fact, he was projecting that the stock, then at about 20, would sell in the low 60's in a matter of time. His logic was reasonable and convincing. He made sense. I agreed that it looked like he sure had a good stock. All he had to do was sit back and wait.

In about 15 minutes a block of this stock crossed on the tape. It was a down tick and he frowned. Then another block of selling, and another. That did it. In a flash the doctor sprinted over to his broker and told him to sell all of his holdings in this stock — at the market!

In less than 30 minutes time, this man went from being a long term, constructive investor to a tape trader! The two don't mix. If you trade by the fundamentals, stick to them. Don't try to overlap another discipline and then expect that you can function between the two opposing thoughts and goals.

44

Christ is supposed to have told another doctor, "Physician, heal thyself." I'm certain that if he had given market advice to any trader or investor it would have been, "Speculator, know thyself."

Until you know yourself and your investment goals, you will not know how to approach the stock market. This means you must stop to think about your entire way of living. How much time do you have to devote to the market? How much time do you want to devote to the market?

How much money do you have? If you are working with limited capital, you do not want to be a short term trader. How much emotional stress and strain can you take? Does you current job permit you to get market quotations during the day? Are you comfortable buying on margin and trading? Are you too nervous to sit on "long term holdings?"

When you have the answers to these questions you can then start to decide what aspect of the market you are going to work with.

HOW TO FORECAST SHORT TERM MOVES

Short term market forecasting is the most difficult due to the wildly erratic swings of short term action. There are, however, certain tools of the trade that usually will enable one to spot the short term buy and sell points with a high degree of accuracy.

These tools are only of value to the short term trader or person who has the time for a closer view of market action. They are not needed by all speculators. You intermediate and long term investors may want to follow one short term index, just to help you spot the very best timing. By and large, however, they are not needed by the average investor.

There are an average of 12 short term up or down moves per year. Thus, your exposure to market risk is greater in that you have more decisions to make. There is more chance for error.

MY FAVORITE SHORT TERM INDICES

I attempt to eliminate as many errors as possible by waiting for two developments to occur before I take any short term action. The developments are:
1. A SHORT TERM OVER-EXTENDED MARKET
2. A TREND REVERSAL SIGNALED BY THE MOMENTUM INDEX

Chart 23

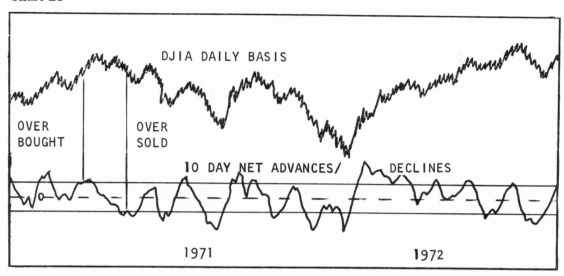

DJIA DAILY BASIS

OVER
BOUGHT

OVER
SOLD

10 DAY NET ADVANCES/ DECLINES

1971   1972

HOW TO TELL WHEN THE MARKET HAS REACHED A SHORT TERM OVERBOUGHT/SOLD POINT

When I first began publishing my advisory service there were no others offering short term market timing. Now, there are a great many, most of which were started by attendees of my seminars. Everyone, including myself, spent many manhours trying to develop a perfect, all-encompassing short term market timing tool. After three years of conducting my own research, swappig indices with others and paying through the nose for "secrets", I came to the realization there are no perfect short term timing tools. They all have their downfalls. In fact, relying upon a perfectly mechanical index is usually the worst thing you can do.

It's a great deal like painting a picture. The world's worst artist will not paint a good picture simply because he has the world's best sable brushes.

The most important aspect of market timing is to have an understanding of where the market has been and where it can go. The lack of this knowledge results in the most common mistake made by investors — that of buying or selling too soon. Your broker, advisor, friend or "trusty" newspaper may tell you the market is oversold, and therefore ready to be bought. But is it really? How do they know? How can you know?

I believe the best indication of overbought/oversold markets comes from a careful study of a 10 day moving average of the number of advancing and declining stocks and a 10 day moving average of a gem of a gauge called the Trading Index.

46

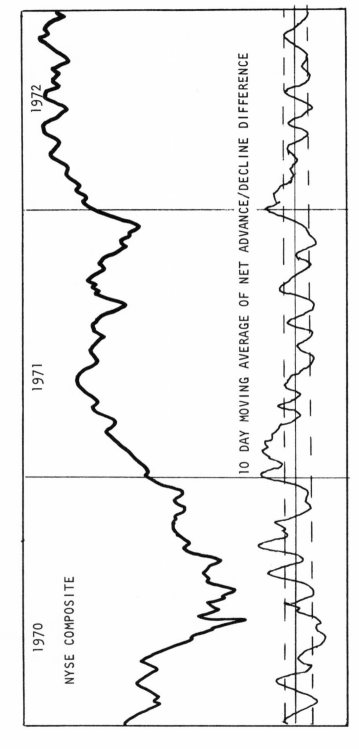

Chart 24

1970   1971   1972

NYSE COMPOSITE

10 DAY MOVING AVERAGE OF NET ADVANCE/DECLINE DIFFERENCE

As the charts show, the 10 day moving average of the net difference between advancing and declining stocks does a rather remarkable job of indicating general areas from where one should be able to expect market reversals. This index is constructed by taking the difference between a 10 day moving average of advancing stocks and a 10 day moving average of declining stocks. The resulting figure will be a plus and plotted above the zero line when the 10 day up stock figure is the larger of the two. When the 10 day down stock figure is larger, the figure will be a minus and plotted below the zero line.

An oversold market is indicated when this index falls below 2,000. An overbought market is signaled by the index rising above — and then falling back below — 1,000. The sole purpose of this gauge is to tell us whether the market is overbought or oversold on a short term basis.

Another way of identifying short term overbought/oversold areas requires a bit more math, but it does a far better job. This method involves use of the Trading Index which is the ratio of up-down volume to up-down stocks.

The index is constructed in three steps. Begin by dividing the number of declining stocks for the day into the number of advancing stocks. This gives you the ratio of up to down stocks. Then divide the amount of declining volume into the amount of advancing volume for an up/down volume ratio.

The Trading Index is then constructed by dividing the volume ratio into the stock ratio. The resulting number will oscillate from a very bullish reading in the low .40's to a very bearish reading above 2.00. I construct this index at the close of trading each day. You can also get the index on the Ultronics machine by punching out STKS, then hitting volume. On the Bunker Ramo machine, ask for MKDS. That will save you the mathematics.

The final step is to run a 10 day moving average of the Trading Index. It will rise and fall from a very high 1.30 area to the very low .80 area.

A short term oversold market is indicated when the 10 day Trading Index rises above .99. An overbought index reading is given when the Trading Index falls below .90. A study of the chart will show the significance of the Trading Index.

Chart 24-A

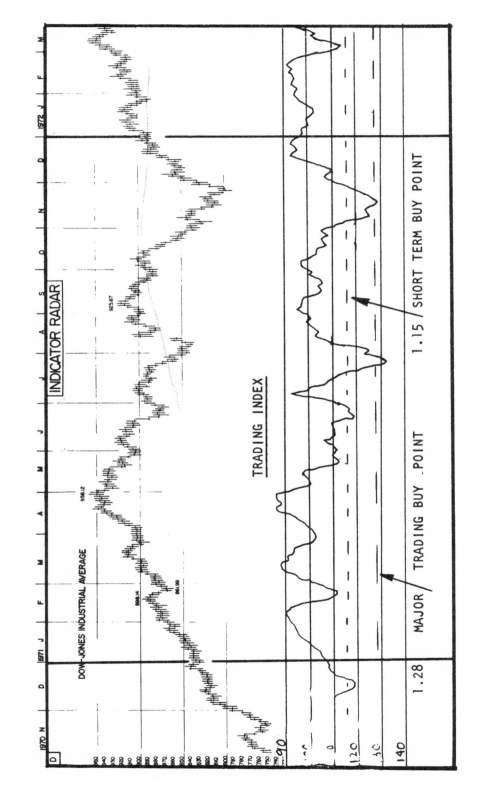

49

WHEN TO TAKE ACTION

Now that you know how to spot the short term overbought and oversold areas, it's time to learn when to enter the market . . . to operate on your own buy/sell signal system.

My studies indicate the very best possible time to take short term market action occurs when the market's short term flow of momentum has convincingly reversed itself. These same studies show that these momentum tools generally top and bottom before the market itself does. Like anything, the momentum tools can be whipsawed. However, the vast majority of the whipsaws are eliminated if we first wait for the market to give an oversold/bought reading. When such readings occur, reversals in the momentum index give very good timing signals.

AN EXPLANATION OF THE MOMENTUM INDEX

Don't let the term "momentum index" scare you away . . . you already know how to construct it! Really. You see, the **10** day net difference between advancing and declining stocks is an accurate reflection of market momentum. This means all you need to do is observe the **10** day Advancing/Declining stock oscillator to see if it reverses its trend at times you have labeled as being overbought or oversold. That's all there is to it!

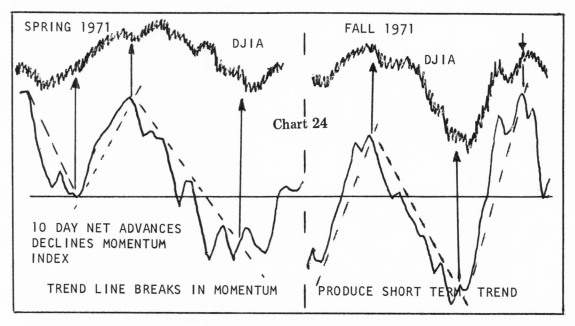

To help you get a better feel for this concept I'm giving you some real closeups on market timing so you can see how useful the momentum index — **10** day net stock data— can be in spotting market reversals.

50

Buying and selling points can also be given when the 10 day Trading Index gauge breaks above or below its trend as shown on the short term market timing charts. It is important that you notice how the 10 day Trading Index gauge frequently gives signals in spite of a falling market. When this index has formed a well-defined trend, a reversal of this trend gives excellent market signals.

HOW TO FORECAST INTERMEDIATE TERM MOVES

Forecasting intermediate term moves is simplest because there are only two or three intermediate term market reversals in a year. This compares with perhaps ten to fifteen short term market reversals! As you can see, the odds favor working the intermediate term trends of the market. The same basic Yin/Yang principles apply here, but we can introduce some additional timing tools to tell us when the market has reached an extreme up or down point.

The one trying thing about calling intermediate term market moves is that you must continually maintain certain data, almost always on a weekly basis, but for all your work you only get to use it a couple of times a year! This causes most people to jump the gun on their indicators and gets them buying or selling too soon. I know from personal experience!

MY FAVORITE INTERMEDIATE TERM INDICES

I have found three very reliable intermediate term timing tools. The first one measures the difference between the yield on stocks and bonds . . . the second follows the trading index and the third one is based on the overbought/oversold indices. All three are good, and, combined they are even better. When three out of three signal a top or bottom, you are really playing the market with a stacked deck.

WHERE WILL THE MARKET GO? — "WILL GO" KNOWS!

The first intermediate term index I want to introduce you to is the one I call "Will-Go" because it tells where the market will go over the intermediate term. In fact, it tells us about ten weeks in advance of the market actually doing it!

This invaluable index is constructed by taking the differences between this week's yield spread between stocks and bonds and the same spread five weeks ago. The yield spread figure is available in Barron's under the Market Laboratory section, third column over, as shown here.

NT • MARKET L

Week's Market Statistics

		Last week	Prev. week	Last year
'g.				
86	Sales NYSE, th shs	61,367	82,529	62,876
22	Sales ASE, th shs	16,188	21,786	17,343
29	Dow-Jones groups:			
72	65 Stks, th shs	7,352	10,133	7,819
	30 Ind, th shs	4,458	6,113	4,272
07	20 Transp, th shs	1,771	2,411	2,432
22	15 Util, th shs	1,123	1,609	1,115
23	20 Most Active Stocks:			
01	Average price	34.75	30.88	35.24
26	Ratio vol to tot vol,%	13.78	13.78	12.91
-	Stock offerings in $	155,790		
s	Bk clrgs, NYC, mil $-v	128,120	115,840	70,810
2	Barron's 10 Hi-Gr			
3	bond yields-v	7.26	7.27	7.62
1	Spread between yields for			
1	Barron's Hi-Gr Bonds			
6	& D-J Ind Stk Avg.	—4.01	—4.05	—4.19
0	Ratio to D-J 40 Bonds			
7	(confidence Index)	95.2	95.0	95.5
0	Prices and Yields (which include stock dividends) on Dow-Jones Averages:			
	30 Ind	961.39	971.25	922.15
0	30 Ind, %	3.25	3.22	3.43
5	20 Transp	253.84	261.06	225.69
9	20 Transp, %	3.01	2.92	3.79
6	15 Util	107.87	108.16	114.33
e	15 Util, %	6.15	6.13	5.67
-	40 Bonds, %-v	7.63	7.65	7.98
	10 Hi Gr, %-v	8.51	8.43	8.57
	10 2d Gr. %-v	8.74	8.85	9.17
	10 Ind, %-v	6.96	6.97	7.25

Just find the difference between this week's value and the value of five weeks ago. If this week's value is greater than five weeks ago you have a plus number. If less than five weeks ago, you have a negative number. Then run a cumulative flow line just as we do with the Accumulation/Distribution line. Add this week's value if it is positive, or subtract it if it's negative and continue doing this each week.

Then plot this index on chart paper. I plot it with a lead time of ten weeks. As you can see on the chart there, Will-Go is plotted in advance of the actual market action. Thus we can see about when the market should top and bottom. You will also notice on the chart that Will-Go has a rather remarkable record for calling the tops and bottoms.

Don't forget that when you see Will-Go topping at the same time as the market, it was actually indicated ten weeks in advance. The top or bottom in Will-Go does not occur at the same time as the market ... it occurs prior to the market's action.

This is a good general index to give you an indication of the most probable direction of an intermediate term move and the time period involved. It will treat you well.

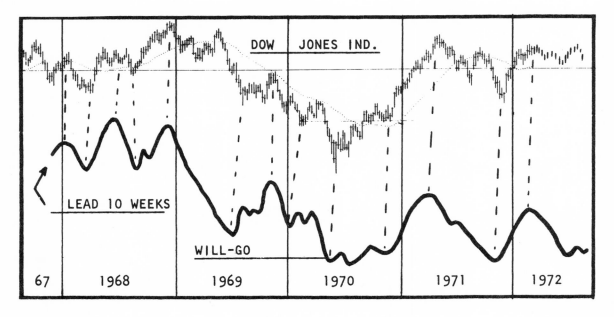

DOW JONES IND.

LEAD 10 WEEKS

WILL-GO

67   1968   1969   1970   1971   1972

Chart 25

YIN AND YANG, REVISITED

Will-Go tells in advance when the market should reverse itself. To supplement this, you need something to assure you that the market has reached an overbought or oversold area of intermediate term significance.

I could give you any number of indices. However, they would only serve to clutter up your thinking and increase the amount of work you'd have to do. This is unnecessary, especially since we can use a ten day moving average of the trading index to tell us when the market has reached an oversold area of some significance for the intermediate term.

An intermediate term market bottom is signaled when the ten day trading index dips into the 130 area.

This doesn't happen very often ... but when it does, you must force yourself to become a buyer of common stocks, especially if Will-Go has told you to expect a market reversal on the upside at this time. The two indices work hand in glove.

Intermediate term tops are practically non-existent in that tops seem to be either short term in duration (we've covered this), or long term, . . and that's covered in the next chapter. For the most part, you want to concentrate on buying stocks that:

1. Have the accumulation price pattern, and
2. Demonstrate aggressive accumulation in the A/D line.

The stocks you have chosen should then be bought at the beginning of a market rally, as indicated by Will-Go, and at the same time that an intermediate market bottom has been confirmed by a trading index reading in the 130 area or higher.

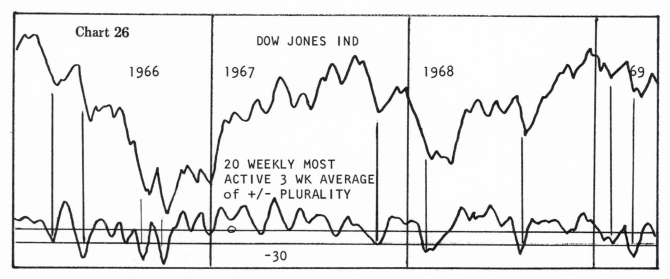

A FINAL INTERMEDIATE TERM INDEX

For those of you not wanting to work with daily figures there is still one more superb intermediate term index which will help you spot the intermediate buying junctures. This index is constructed with the week's most active stocks, as reported in most all Sunday papers. It is basically an overbought/oversold index.

Add up the number of the most actives that were up for the week and the number that were off for the week. Let's say 17 were up and three were down. This would give you a net reading of +14. If there were 6 stocks up and 14 stocks down for the week, the net reading would be −12. Do this for each week's market and then run a three week moving average of the weekly net +/− figure of the 20 most actives.

As the chart of the 20 most actives shows, very good buying junctures are clearly announced when this index falls below a three week average of −30 or more. Very important market bottoms are signaled by readings below −40 where smart speculators mortgage their homes for an intermediate term rally — even in Bear markets!

CHAPTER 6

HOW CYCLES CAN IMPROVE YOUR STOCK TIMING

HOW CYCLES CAN IMPROVE YOUR STOCK TIMING

For many years some of the street's most astute minds have tried to crack the mystery behind market cycles. There are several good publications, notably "Cycles," published by the Foundation for the Study of Cycles, that continually report on cyclical phenomena.

These people seek to put all market action into one or two cyclical patterns. To them, a perfect cycle is a move composed of two equal movements. As the illustration show, the up and down leg of the cycle are equal. It is also important to note that the depth or magnitude of the cycle is equal to the length of the cycle. This will always hold true in a perfect cycle. This tells us that if the last cycle had a duration of 22 days, so will the next if the pattern is to repeat itself.

Even more significant is the fact that if we believe a cycle is half way through we can then extend the length of the first leg and project where the second leg of the cycle should most probably end.

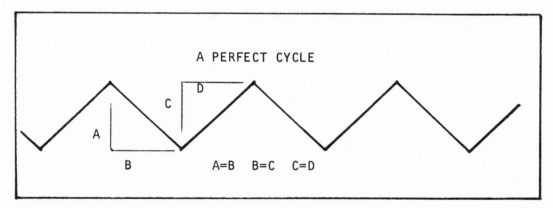

Chart 27

The above method works pretty well...except for one thing...there are precious few perfect cycles in the stock market. I think this is where the cycle boys have missed the boat. They expect too much from an imperfect discipline. The market or individual stocks do not move in uniform cycles. Not at all. They move in cyclical patterns. That's the secret of understanding this area of market behavior.

THE SECRET OF IDENTIFYING INDIVIDUAL STOCK TRADING PATTERNS

I try to identify what cyclical pattern the stocks I follow are in. This is done in a most crude way. I simply make note of where all important lows on the chart have taken place.

The next step is to measure this distance from one low to the next. I find that most lows are close to being an equal distance apart. If the last two lows were 27 days apart, I am convinced that the next low of the magnitude I am measuring will come 27 days after the most recent low.

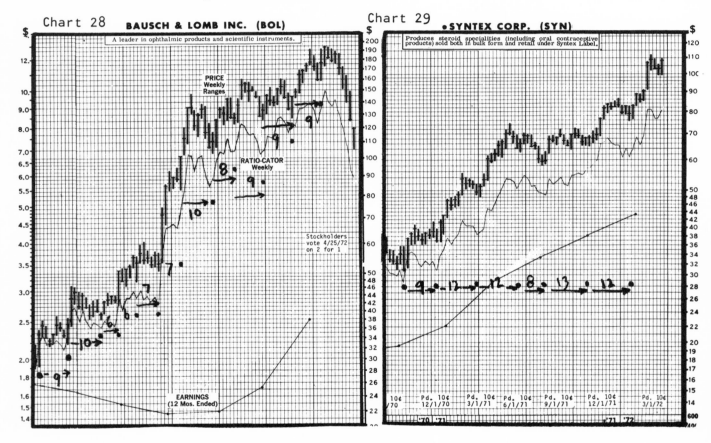

All my computer programming and research has not produced a better method for identifying an individual stock's cyclical pattern.

Once this is done, you must continually up-date your study to see if the cycle is changing as well as re-adjust the projected low point which might result from a price overshoot or undershoot some place along the way.

The illustrations shown cover this point much better than I can. It's important for you to keep in mind that patterns are not perfect and are subject to change. Their purpose is to fine-tune your timing and to keep you from getting in too early.

IDENTIFYING THE PATTERNS

There are two basic patterns you will see in all individual stock behavior. One consists of a long up move and short down move while the other reverses this pattern seeing a short up move and a long down or sideways action. One or the other pattern is usually repeated in cadence and continues to be operative in the stock for many, many years.

Some stocks are extremely responsive to their pattern. Burroughs is a good example. The stock trades in a well-defined pattern of 10 weeks on the upside and 4 weeks down. The 10 week advance phase has an up, down, up move riding on top of the extended 10 week up leg. This, too, is easier to discern from the chart than it is to comprehend in words.

Chart 30

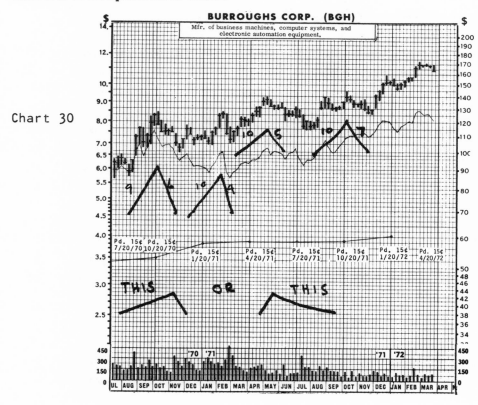

HOW TO USE THIS INFORMATION

Once you have isolated and identified the patterns influencing your stock's behavior, the data can be used in one of two ways. The most basic is simply to note on your chart, as already discussed, where the next low point should be. This is done by extending the cycle from the last well-identified low point. This works well for bottoms, but not as well for tops. It will help spot some tops, but not all. It is less precise than the bottom finding technique.

57

MEASURING THE CYCLE'S MOMENTUM

Recently, several books have appeared on the scene offering to tell investors how to track stock cycles. I've read the books and found the information to be good, but the approach is so time consuming that it is of little value. You see, cycles are just one small part of a stock's action. A stock may be in a perfect cycle, as in the example shown here, but if professional accumulation does not come in at the turning point of the cycle, there will be only a small rally, if any.

You must continually check with our other tools to see if the cycle is still in gear and ready for a decent up or down leg. Cyclical phenomena alone will not rapidly influence the price structure. It must come at a time when the accumulation distribution studies are also in gear with the cycle.

The more mathematically inclined among you can use the basic cyclical information to construct gauges to measure the strength and weakness of the cycle.

This is done by running a rate of change of the stock's closing price. The length of the rate of change is based on the cycle. It is a 22 day cycle, you will want to use an 11 day rate of change. A 50 day cycle needs a 25 day rate of change, etc.

The total number of trading days from low to low is the cycle's length. You measure the rate of change from a time period ½ the length of the cycle. This is done so you can capitalize on both the up and down leg of the cycle. This gives you short term magnification for maximum profits as the momentum data clearly shows both legs developing.

When the momentum index breaks above its longer term trend lines, buy signals are given. Sell signals are given when the momentum line falls below its long term trend line. Again, check the illustration to get a better understanding of the use of the momentum indices. Also, note that two different indices are used, a 25 day for NOM and a 17 day for BGH. All stocks are not in the same pattern.

In case you've forgotten, a rate of change is constructed by taking the difference between today's closing price and the closing price of X days ago. The price difference, plus or minus, is then plotted in a plus or minus fashion above and below a zero line. You can see how this has been done for NOM & BGH.

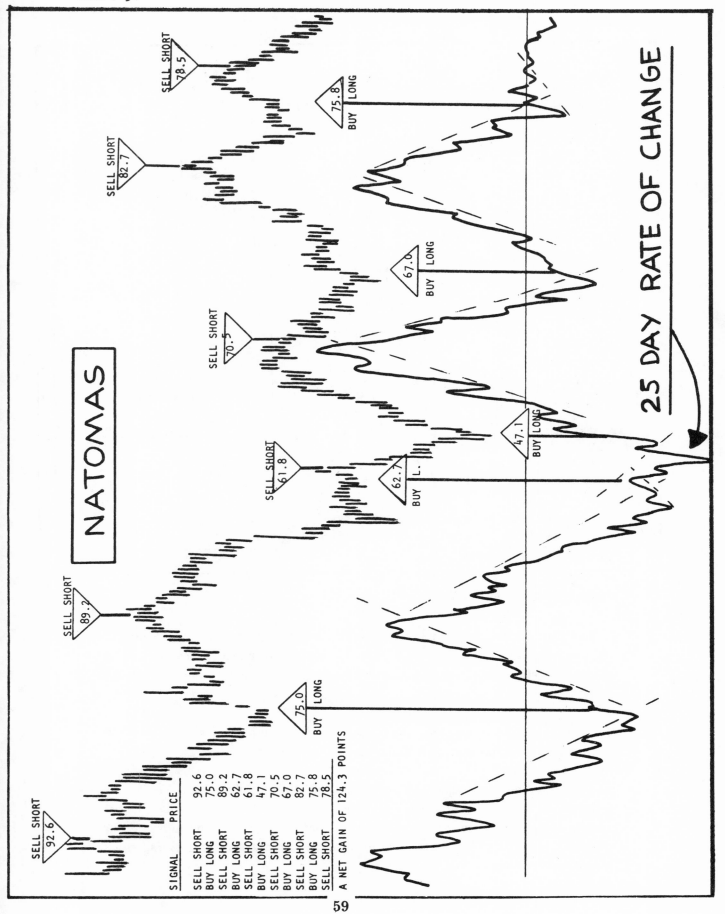

Chart 31

NATOMAS

SIGNAL	PRICE
SELL SHORT	92.6
BUY LONG	75.0
SELL SHORT	89.2
BUY LONG	62.7
SELL SHORT	61.8
BUY LONG	47.1
SELL SHORT	70.5
BUY LONG	67.0
SELL SHORT	82.7
BUY LONG	75.8
SELL SHORT	78.5

A NET GAIN OF 124.3 POINTS

25 DAY RATE OF CHANGE

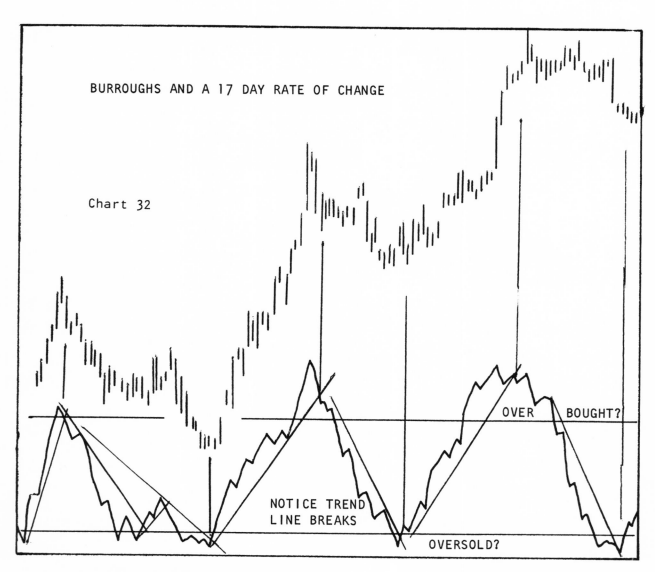

BURROUGHS AND A 17 DAY RATE OF CHANGE

Chart 32

NOTICE TREND LINE BREAKS

OVER BOUGHT?

OVERSOLD?

PRECISION TIMING WITH CYCLES

In summation then, we see that cycles can be useful to give us advance warning of the potential area where, in terms of time, we should expect prices to reverse themselves, etc. This serves as a guide to trading and keeps us from jumping the gun.

To avoid waiting too long we construct the momentum indices which clearly tell us when the cycle has bottomed and a new move is underway.

Neither method forecasts the duration of the coming leg... only the approximate reversal point. Do not expect a move of any consequence just because the cyclical pattern has been met. Major money making moves occur when the patterns are in phase with professional accumulation and overall stock market bullishness.

POLITICS AND THE MARKET

Regardless of how you feel about the powers to be in the White House, now or 20 years from now, there are some interesting lessons to learn from studying the relationship of presidential terms and stock market activity.

The most apparent relationship, one few if any are aware of, is the overwhelming evidence that the first year in office for a President produces a down market.

Historical records show the market has averaged a 1.2% loss in all the years a president began a new term. This is the weakest year of the four year term. More significantly, all of the major Bear markets since 1936 have begun during this ill fated first year in office!

Chart
33

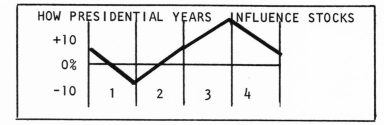

As a president's second year in office begins, things start to get a little better and the market has shown advances averaging almost 8% during the second year.

The fireworks start to explode in a President's third year in office. This is highlighted by the astounding average gain of over 16% for the third year in office.

In the fourth and final year of the term, prices still tend to post gains, but not as substantially as those seen in the second and the third year of the term.

The chart shows how the average predental term affects the market. Your own memory of President Nixon's first year in office, a total disaster for the market, should serve to jog your memory whenever a new presidential term begins.

The statistic validity of the impact of presidential years is high. In the first year category, there have been 5 declines in 9 terms of office. At first glance, this does not appear decisively bearish, but when you consider the long term trend has been up, it takes on more significance.

The strongly bullish third year category has seen seven advances out of 8 terms of office. Six of the seven advances posted gains greater than 10% for the year. That is highly significant and should become a part of your overall long term investment policy.

CHAPTER 7

WHAT YOU NEED TO KNOW ABOUT

LONG TERM STOCK MARKET

TIMING

WHAT YOU NEED TO KNOW ABOUT LONG TERM STOCK MARKET TIMING

As I've mentioned earlier, your success or failure in the market will be dependent upon your ability to select the right stock at the right time. Stocks under aggressive accumulation cannot be expected to buck a major Bear market. During the course of a major Bull market stocks showing signs of massive distribution will tend to be weaker than the averages, but seldom produce enough weakness to make short selling profitable.

Thus, it is imperative that you have a working idea of whether we are in a major Bull or Bear trend. Once you have determined if the market will be dominated by the Bears you should work the short side of the market. Should your analysis indicate we are in a major Bull move, you'd better forget all about short selling and concentrate on going long.

WHAT A MAJOR MARKET BOTTOM LOOKS LIKE — While a rose, is a rose, is a rose, and most market bottoms look the same, there is not enough similarity that we can identify one pattern and say that is the way all Bull markets begin. Nonetheless, many of the same conditions are present at most Bull market creations . . . enough that when we see the majority of them again appearing it's safe to assume a Bull market is on its way.

The hallmark of most all Bull markets is a selling climax.

HOW TO IDENTIFY A SELLING CLIMAX

Let's take a look at the classical selling climax. As strange as it may seem, most selling climaxes take two days . . . and these two days are almost always a Monday and a Tuesday. Even more interesting is that such climaxes usually come at the end of the month.

There are many good examples of this, some of the best in recent years have been the Monday-Tuesday selling climaxes of; November 22-23, 1971, August 8-9, 1971, May 25-26, 1970, July 28-29, 1969, August 4-5, 1968, March 4-5, 1968 and the text book selling climax of Monday-Tuesday, October 3-4, 1966.

Along with the Monday-Tuesday syndrome, classical selling climaxes have other identifiable characteristics. One method I've devised to help me identify selling climaxes is to simply keep in mind that selling climaxes come at the end of large downmoves. My rule here is that I cannot treat any potential climatic activity as an honest to goodness climax unless the Dow Jones Industrial action has fallen at least **100** points. After that much of a drop you can start expecting a climax . . . until then, be cautious.

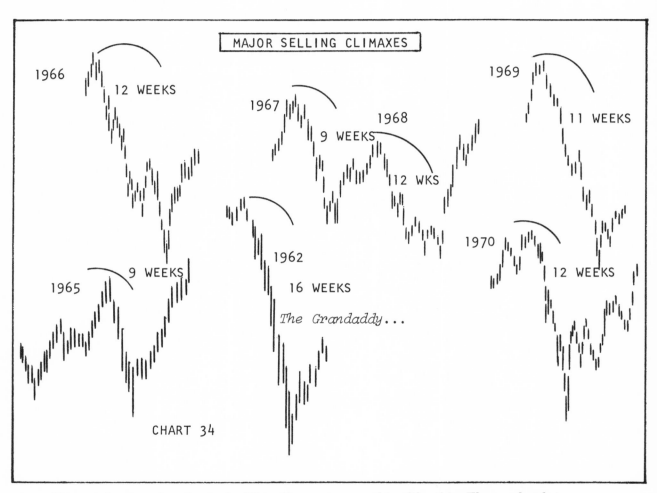

The mechanics of a classical selling climax go something like this: The market has been undergoing massive liquidation. For several weeks the main topic of conversation in the mass media has been the market's inability to rally. Usually the down trend has been in effect for at least 9 weeks. It's been a real nasty tumble.

On a Monday near the end of a month, or the first week of a new month, the market continues plummeting, dropping about 15 Dow points. On Tuesday, the market extends its crash phase breaking below yesterday's low while volume runs at a faster pace than the previous days' efforts.

63

For those that have access to it, the Tick Index should fall below minus 700 at the very bottom of the selling climax.

Then, in almost a flash, and while stocks are trading with a late tape and digits deleted — on the downside — a rally begins that immediately causes the tape to become further behind, but on the upside. This rally gathers momentum and suddenly the Dow is off only a few points for the day. A brief selling wave comes in attempting to knock prices back down, but it fails and the averages zoom up exceeding yesterday's close and ending the day slightly above or below yesterday's high.

That completes the selling climax. It consists of two drastic down days. On the second day prices quickly reverse . . . on a late tape . . . to close up substantially for the day. Some selling climaxes see this same pattern with Tuesday being the real cruncher and prices closing up on Wednesday.

There are some other points of interest to note about the classical selling climaxes. To begin with, they usually occur at what the chartists are calling an important support point that, if broken, would lead to disasterously lower prices.

Secondly, the climax rally should come after there have been at least two, and ideally three, other short term rally attempts that have failed since the overall selling wave began.

Notice on the chart how the selling wave sees numerous attempts to rally but all fail. Thus, when the climax comes those who have been "sucked in" before refuse to follow the reversal and even sell it short, as informed investors take down all the stock they can get their hands on.

WHAT A MAJOR TOP LOOKS LIKE — While major bottoms are marked by gigantic selling climaxes that spin the long term tide from bearish to bullish in almost a split second, market tops tend to be long drawn out affairs. Because of this, I've coined a little maxim to help in long term timing:
"Be quick to turn bullish, slow to turn bearish."

Market tops seem to come in two versions in terms of their appearance on the charts. The first is one I call a "stop and go" top, the other a "double top."

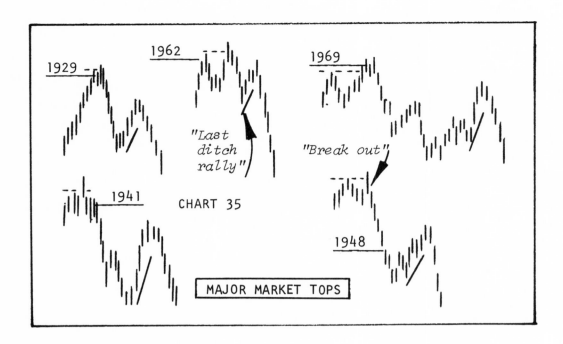

The "stop and go" top is a real fooler . . . especially to the chartists. Its pattern is one where prices have been rallying strongly for the last 12 months. Then a very strong rally comes in lifting just about all stocks and creating hefty profits . . . on paper . . . for all hands in the game. Then there is a brief pullback and a flashy rally breaking out above the old peak. To the novice, it looks like he's suddenly found a money making machine. Bulls are everywhere and the few remaining Bears throw in the towel because of the break out to new highs.

Then one bright chipper morning, usually a Thursday, prices stage a big run up, but fail to hold their gains. The next day, Friday, sees a "surprising" decline and by the time Monday's market has closed there's been a real break in the price structure of the averages and most all stocks.

Market tops are very difficult to identify. This it true partly because of the long duration and partly because tops are made as prices break to new highs. Logically the break to new highs should produce even higher prices and is very difficult to get bearish about. But close study of major market tops shows they almost always come immediately after a break to new rally highs!

In the event you fail to notice the actual market top, there's always one more chance to get out before the real serious damage is done by the rampaging Bears. This last chance to bail out usually occurs about 3 months after the major top has been formed. The pattern is one where prices break badly from the major market top and decline for almost 1½ months. Then an intermediate term rally begins that most people wrongly call the start of a new Bull move. It isn't! It's just the opportunity to do your final selling as prices rally back towards the original high point.

Seldom is this high point reached . . . the rally is strictly a false rally and can be easily identified as such by 1. a weak showing in the daily advance decline line, 2. the fact heavy resistance enters as prices move back toward their 200 day moving average lines and 3. short selling done by members of the Exchange becomes quite large as the rally progresses.

This "last ditch" rally usually ends on a Monday as prices open up extending the previous Friday's gains. The first two or three hours of the day see some sizeable moves. But suddenly, selling forces enter and drive prices down, closing the averages below yesterday's close.

Notice how our chart depicts this last ditch rally as a move lasting about half as long as the down move from the important top.

TWO FUNDAMENTAL INDICATORS TO SPOT MARKET TOPS — To some extent, fundamentals can help us identify times when stocks are under or over valued and a major change in direction is inevitable. The fundamental figures I'm talking about are the yields on Standard and Poor's 500 and the annualized rate of change of money supply.

As mentioned in Chapter One, stock yields can be tremendously helpful in telling us when a stock is over valued. In terms of the market average, the same thing holds true. The problems here have been, in recent years, just what average to follow. The DJIA has been a lethargic average, thus its yield has not been as low as the more volatile Standard and Poor's 500 Index.

For my money, I'd rather follow the yield on the S&P 500 stocks than the popular, but limited in scope, 30 Dow Jones Industrial issues.

As a rule of thumb, you should expect a Bear market to begin anytime the yield on the S&P 500 falls below 2.8%. This does not mean that a Bear market will immediately follow such a low reading, but it does mean that such readings indicate you are very close to the start of a major Bear market.

The long term history of the S&P Yield shows just about all major Bear markets since the early 1900's have begun when this or similiar indices were less than 2.8%. Readings in this area should beam out rays of caution to you.

Unfortunately, the yield information is not as helpful at market bottoms as at market tops. This is a one sided index in that it's main purpose is to identify areas of selling, not buying.

HOW MONEY SUPPLY CAN HELP YOU — To stimulate or sedate our economy, the Federal Reserve System alters the growth rate of the amount of money in circulation. This is done in a variety of ways. The most common is by influencing the currency plus demand deposit figures.

Well . . I can't go along with them quite that far from the research I've done. For one thing, money supply and its followers have missed some very important market tops and bottoms. Secondly, my money supply data shows several times when money supply expanded rapidly but stock prices continued falling. The 1929 crash was one such time!

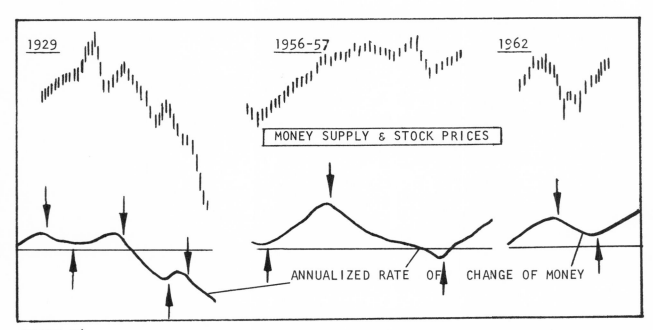

CHART 36

Money supply usually, but not always, tops and bottoms in advance of stock market peaks and valleys. The key thing here is in determining just how long of a lead time money supply has over stock market prices.

The 1962 Bear market was not called by the money supply figures because there was no real decline in money supply and what little dip there was occurred at the same time as the market break. However, most students of money supply say that money supply tops out 12-16 months in advance of stocks.

To my way of thinking, that's a bit too much of a variable in lead time. Hence, I treat money supply in a slightly different manner. My approach is one wherein I monitor many long term indices. Each month I note how many are bullish or bearish and when the majority of them are bullish so am I. When the majority of them turn bearish, Larry Williams follows with chameleon like quickness.

Thus, money supply is just one index to watch and keep track of. When it turns positive or negative it's just an indication of future market action, not a mandate for a sudden reversal.

When the annualized rate of change turns negative (see chapter 6 to learn how to construct rates of change) I become cautious immediately. When the annualized rate of change becomes positive, I start becoming bullish but am in no hurry to cover all my shorts because money supply usually bottoms 3-6 months before stock market prices.

Remember, money supply is not, to my knowledge, a fine tuning index. At its best it appears to be an index helpful in identifying areas of economic growth or restraint that will take its toll on stock market prices at some point in the future. It is not a guarantee of future market action, merely a hint of probable happenings.

THREE TECHNICAL INDICATORS TO SPOT MAJOR TOPS — While calling major market tops is an admittedly difficult task, there are some indices that can make that task much easier.   By and large, it is my conviction that technical indicators are more helpful in pinpointing major stock market tops and bottoms than their fundamental counterparts.

Effective long term major indices for spotting tops usually work because they reflect excessive public participation, and a lack of money specifically earmarked for stocks. Three such indicators are presented here.

If I had only one long term index to use it would be the annualized rate of change of the total monthly short positions.

Let me start by saying this index is not one of my inventions. It is the product of the remarkably creative Dr. Roy Christian of Aptos, California. Dr. Christian found that when the annualized rate of change for the total monthly short position changed from being positive to negative, very good stock market sell signals were given. When the annualized rate of change switched from negative to positive, superb long term buy signals were given.

This index works because it reflects when too many people are too bearish or too bullish. The monthly short position is an approximate representation of how much short selling has been done in the market. When there's been too much short selling, i.e., the annualized rate of change of the short positions is positive, it's time to buy long. This is a contrary indicator, one that tells us what the crowd is doing so we can do just the opposite.

The New York Stock Exchange releases the short position about the 20th of each month. I do not use the short interest ratio, but the total short position.

The long term chart shows how accurate this index has been during the last 31 years of market history. It has a superb record of defining, often in advance, major Bull and Bear markets.

Another approach to the market focuses on the activity of the mutual funds. Since figures were first available for these influential investors, one thing has been established: When funds are low on cash stocks go down until the funds are cash heavy and then stocks advance!

The trick here is establishing just what are low and high levels of cash. It is difficult because there are several parameters to the fund cash picture. For one thing, the funds have a continual problem of redemption, money being withdrawn by shareholders as well as incoming monies from recent fund holder purchases. Along with this there is the funds' monthly cash position which can be ratioed to their total assets. By doing that we have a figure telling us what percent of the funds' money is invested.

To correctly view all these figures, I run a 12 month moving sum of the funds redemptions and compare it to the most recent month's cash position. This then compares the amount of money on hand versus the amount of money being called away from the funds. When the 12 month sum of redemptions exceeds the monthly cash position a sell signal is given as long as the percent of cash to assets is less than 5.0%.

For a feel of this gauges' accuracy, please carefully study the long term 31 year history chart for the actual sell and buy signals.

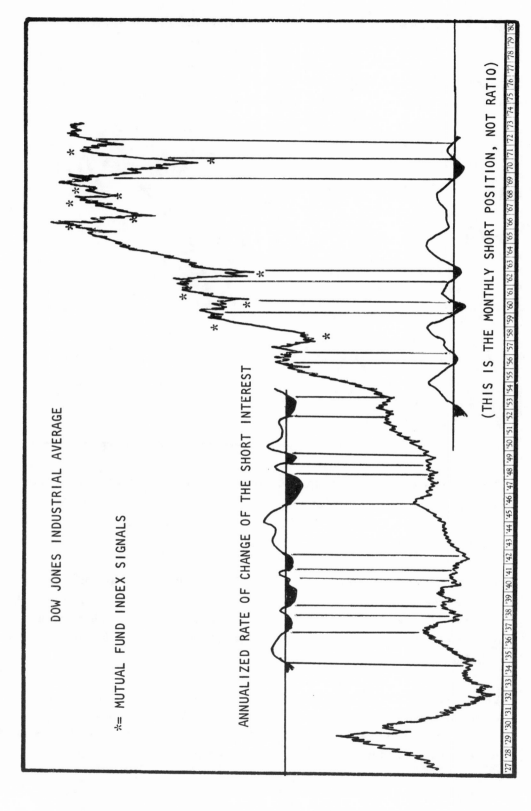

Chart 37

DOW JONES INDUSTRIAL AVERAGE

*= MUTUAL FUND INDEX SIGNALS

ANNUALIZED RATE OF CHANGE OF THE SHORT INTEREST

(THIS IS THE MONTHLY SHORT POSITION, NOT RATIO)

70

A third technical sign that stock prices are in danger has been when a disparity has been created between the advance decline line and the Dow Jones Industrial Average. By disparity I'm referring to the type of market that sees the DJIA move to a new Bull market high while the daily, or weekly, line of cummulative advances and declines fails to move to a similar high.

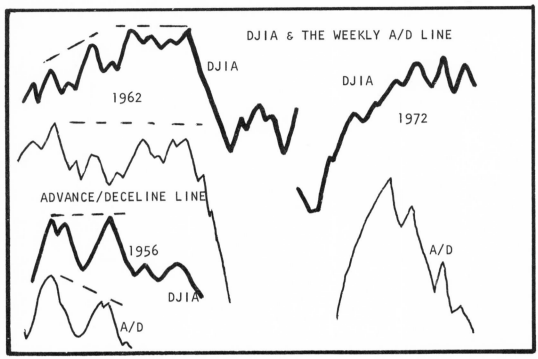

Chart 38

The advance decline line is simple to construct. You merely add all of todays advancing stocks to your line or base figure and subtract all of todays declining issues. This creates a line that represents the action of all stocks traded on the board, unweighted by price.

Almost without exception market tops have seen divergence between this invaluable measurement of total stock market breadth and the averages. It's really a sign that while the averages are being used to advertise and attract more buyers only a few stocks are strong while the majority are under professional distribution.

I'm showing here several examples of major stock market tops so you can see for yourself how reliable the advance decline line is. The few times the A/D line diverged from the market and a Bear market didn't follow occurred at times my other technical and fundamental indicators were strongly bullish.

Incidentally, this index cannot be used to spot major market bottoms as there is seldom any divergence at market bottoms between the averages and the A/D.

HOW TO CALL A MAJOR STOCK MARKET BOTTOM — I've done it and so can you. Spotting major market bottoms is not nearly as hard as spotting the tops. Calling the bottom can be aided by waiting until a select few indices turn bullish and then waiting for a selling climax at which point you go 100% long.

With the exception of money supply figures and various interest rate trends, it's my opinion that fundamental indicators cannot identify major stock market bottoms. This is particularly due to the fact that fundamental or economic indices are usually reported monthly or quarterly and hence are delayed. And finally, we cannot forget that the stock market is itself a leading indicator of the economy. Thus, it's pretty hard to argue that information that follows something else can forecast that "something else".

FOUR INDICATORS TO CALL A MAJOR BOTTOM — The annualized rate of change of the total monthly short position, already discussed for calling major tops, does a splendid job of also calling major market low points. Its historical record is very good. The only questionable signal was its October 1970 buy which came a few months after the actual low was struck. Its performance at the 1949, 1960 and 1962 bottoms more than makes up for the delayed 1970 signal. A buy signal is given when the annualized rate of change turns positive.

Another valuable sentiment indicator is one which measures the amount of short selling being done by members of the New York Stock Exchange. These short sellers represent one of the craftiest and cagiest groups on Wall Street. They are the finest example of big, smart, informed money. Seldom do they miss any important stock market reversals.

We can compare the short sales figures by adding up the amount of shorting being done by Floor Traders, Specialists and other off floor members. Market students are referred to my good friend Wally Hieby's excellent book on the subject, "THE NEW DYNAMIC SYNTHESIS". Short sales figures are released weekly and usually appear in each Thursday's Wall Street Journal. After arriving at the total amount of short selling being done by the members, I divide the member short selling by the total short selling for the reporting week and have the percent of short selling the members are doing.

When the members short selling ratio drops below 65%, a market bottom of at least some significance is close by. When the ratio falls all the way to 55%, it is time to actually mortgage your house, buy long and forget about stop points. The historical record of the members shows them to be by far the most profitable traders in the market. It is essential that you learn to follow these people.

The mutual fund index approach, as I've already discussed, always does a commendable job of giving major market buy points, as the long term chart shows.

The requisites for a major buy signal from this index are that the funds must be very heavy on cash to the point that their cash to asset position is greater than 7%. Secondly, the amount of cash reserves must be at least 120% greater than the 12 month sum of redemptions. This percent figure is arrived at by dividing the 12 month redemption figure into the fund's cash reserves. Once this resulting ratio is greater than 120%, a major Bull market should be in the hibernation stages.

Data for the mutual funds is released monthly by the Mutual Fund Institute and appears in the Wall Street Journal, Barron's and other financial publications.

Another nifty little index to call major stock market bottoms, since data was first available in the 1960's, is the number of secondary issues being offered by the brokerage firms. A secondary is an offering by a company to sell more of their stock. In other words, it's an attempt by the insiders to get out of their corporate stock. As you might suspect, a large number of such secondaries usually spells disaster for the market. The problem is that the large number of secondaries may come along in advance of the actual market high.

To measure the secondaries' activity, I use a 4 week moving sum of the number of secondaries as reported each week in Barron's. When the 4 week moving sum falls under 5, you'd better get ready for some explosive action on the upside because a Bull market is just a few weeks away.

The secondary index, like all the other ones mentioned in this chapter do not flash signals every week or two. These are long term indices that may give signals only once in the next two or three years dependent upon market conditions.

Because of that factor, some people who follow these indices do not act upon them when the signals actually come, or worse yet, they try to second guess the index and jump ahead of actual signals. Please don't do that. Wait for the signal. After all, why should you try to tell the market or an index what it's going to do?

Again, I caution you not to rely solely upon any one of the indices I've given you here despite the obvious good record they have. Instead, I'd prefer that you keep track of all of them and wait for the majority of the Bull market indices to turn positive before buying. Bear market tops can be forecast in the same manner if you'll just wait until the majority, more than 50%, of the Bear market indices turn negative. Once that happens, it's safe to enter the short side of the market and sell out your long positions.

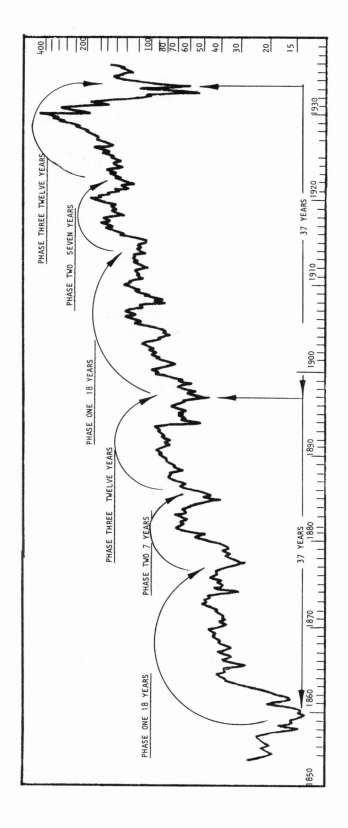

Chart 39

THE STOCK MARKET'S MASTER CYCLICAL PATTERN — Many analysts contend there is some sort of master stock market cycle or pattern and I'm inclined to go along with this point of view. What I'm not inclined to go along with is that one can profitably trade the market using just these long term master cycles.

I'm going to show you here the long term master cycle I have discovered. It's a dandy and is the best cyclical example of long term market action I have ever seen. But that does not mean I would rush out and buy or sell stocks just because this cyclical pattern was calling for a high or low.

Instead, I would insist that once the cyclical elements begin to shape up for a major top or bottom, that reversal must also be forecast by my technical or fundamental data. Then, and only then, would I step into the market.

In a very real way, I want you to consider the William's Master Stock Market Cycle as a road map of about where the market should be going. That's what it's for . . . to show you the general direction and the general timing of the market's super long term characteristics.

As Spring follows Winter and Life follows Death, all observable behavior can be seen fiting into repetitive patterns. Especially in the stock market! It is my contention that a precisely accurate Master Stock Market Pattern does exist. It is submitted here for your observation.

THE MASTER PATTERN IDENTIFIED — The above chart reflects the Axe-Houghton Industrial Stock Price Average from 1854 through 1896. At first glance little can be seen. However, on closer observation an exciting pattern develops.

The pattern is simple; every 37 years the stock market repeats itself. In other words, the low seen in 1859 is the start of a 37 year pattern expiring in the market low seen in 1896.

Later on, it will be shown that this is, indeed, a repetitive pattern with precision like accuracy. For now though, let me identify the components of the 37 year pattern seen above.

The chart has been marked off to show the three cyclical phases within the 37 year pattern. This was done by starting at the 1859 low. Some 18 years later, another major low is seen in 1877 where phase two comes into existance and lasts until the major low recorded in 1884. At this point the third and final phase of the Master Pattern comes into play lasting until 1896.

The first phase lasted (start to finish or low to low) 18 years. Phase two lasted 7 years and the final phase lasted exactly 12 years giving us a 37 year total.

Additionally,the time lapsed from the beginning of phase one to its zenith was 14 years with a 4 year slide to the 1877 lows. Phase two reached its peak about 5 years after its inception. From there, a two year Bear market unfolded. Phase three took 8 years to reach its top from which another 4 year Bear market began.

Before proceeding further, let me identify these three phases in terms of their time duration, price patterns and general construction. After this, you can check the record of the last 115 years to confirm or deny my Master Pattern thesis.

Chart 40

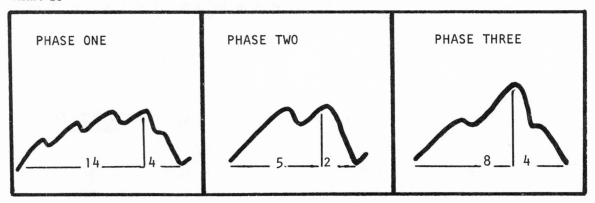

PHASE ONE — This is the first phase of the 37 year pattern. Notice there are 4 "Bull" waves within the context of the overall up trend lasting for 14 years.

In the 14th year, a 4 year Bear market begins, ending the life of this phase.

Important market low points are seen 6, 12, and 15 years from the starting point. Important tops are found 7, 11, and 17 years from the last high point of the previous phase.

PHASE TWO — Here is the shortest of the three phases and the simplest in terms of price structure.

Points of interest are the high seen about 5 years after the start and the ultimate low point 7 years from the starting point.

This pattern calls for a 5 year Bull move, which consists of two up legs with one intervening Bear market. From this high, an approximate two year Bear market begins.

PHASE THREE — This is the third and final phase of the 37 year pattern. The time span from the beginning to the high is 8 years. From this peak a 4 year Bear market begins at which point the 37 year pattern starts all over again.

It is this top, the one 8 years after the third pahse begins, that has produced the major stock market debacles of this country.

Examples of this phase would be the 1884 to 1892 up move, 1921 to 1929 and 1958 to 1966 market.

If there is any validity to my overall thesis we should see market tops and bottoms falling in multiples of 37 years after all the tops and bottoms we have identified in the first 37 year pattern from 1859 to 1896. There are 7 major turning points in the 37 year pattern and 76 years have transpired from 1896, or slightly over 2 complete cycles. Thus, a perfect score would see 14 tops and bottoms falling during the two 37 year cycles after the 1859-96 pattern.

If I get 11 "hits" the method is 80% correct. I will classify a "hit" as any major move coming exactly 37 years, and in multiples thereof, from a corresponding top or bottom already identified in the first 37 year pattern.

A LOOK AT THE RECORD — The phase one move that began in 1859 should, if my theory is valid, produce similar low points every 37 years.

Thus, we add 37 years to 1859 and arrive at 1896, a major market low. To this 37 is added again and we have 1933, the year the advance decline line ended its 1929 Bear market spill! To 1933 we once more add 37 and arrive at 1970 . . . again a perfect hit and forecast. The next similar low should arrive in 2007.

The high point of our original pattern occurred in 1872, so we again add 37 years as stocks made an important high! Next, 1909 plus 37 projects a high for 1946, a brilliant selling point!

Our next point of reference on the orginal pattern is the 1877 low so here we go again: 1877 + 37 = 1914, a major market bottom. Add another 37 and we arrive at 1951, the only miss in the pattern! In actuality, a major low was scored in the later part of 1949 and early 1950, thus, we cannot call this a direct hit, close, but not quite close enough. 1951 + 37 = 1988 for this next low.

Phase two topped out in 1882. Adding 37 years to this forecasts a top in 1919, which is another bulls eye! Toss in another 37 years and we have 1956 — the exact start of a 1.5 year Bear market! The next projection here is for 1993.

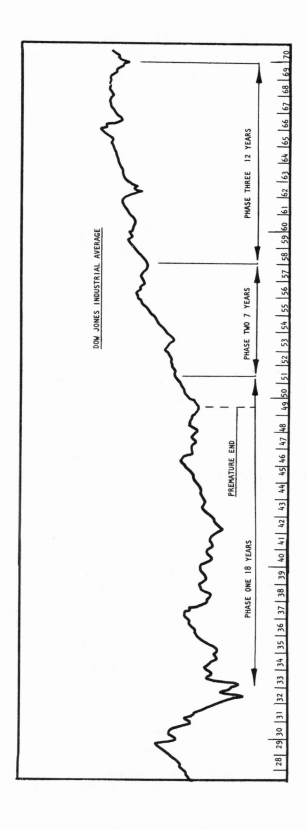

Chart 41

Phase two bottomed out and three began in 1884. This is repetitious, but necessary; we again add 37 to 1884 and can forecast a 1921 low. Did it come about? You bet it did as stocks bottomed and an 8 year Bull market began! To 1921 we add 37 and forecast 1958, another major market low giving birth to an 8 year Bull market culminating in 1966 at DJIA 1000! Our next forecast here calls for a low in 1995.

In 1892 the third phase topped out as prices entered a devastating Bear market. A forecast is made by adding 37 to 1892 and we have . . . 1929. To this we add 37 and have 1966.

Of 14 possible re-occurances, 13 were exactly on schedule. And remember, we have very strict standards of judging "hits". Many observers have been content if a low comes 2 years one way or the other of their long term projection. On that basis, all my projectiosn were correct. As is:
93% OF THE TIME THE PROJECTED MAJOR STOCK MARKET HIGH AND LOWS WERE CORRECT!

Should anyone need further documentation of what I call the WILLIAMS 37 YEAR MASTER STOCK MARKET PATTERN, I would suggest you study other 37 year re-occurring patterns in the averages. They are there. I've only touched on the major ones in this chapter.

Students of cycles will see many of their pet cycles fall into place within the 37 year pattern. In fact, the most common market cycles are the 18 year, 7 year and 12 year cycles, all corresponding with our three phases!

A 35 YEAR STOCK MARKET PROJECTION — Should our 37 year pattern be correct, it will produce a major high in 1983, major low in 1988, major high in 1993, major low in 1995 and a major high (1929 style) in 2003, with a major low in 2007 as the current 37 year pattern draws to a close and another comes to life.

So that you might have a better understanding of this remarkable pattern, I am reproducing here all stock market action from 1854 to date. The similarities are amazing!

It is my belief that the information shared with you in this chapter will enable you to notice important major tops and bottoms with enough accuracy and lead time so that you never again have to worry about being caught by the Bulls or Bears. Follow the indices and you should have little difficulty with your long term market timing.

POINTS TO REMEMBER

1. KEEP A WATCHFUL EYE FOR SELLING CLIMAXES

2. BE QUICK TO TURN BULLISH, SLOW TO TURN BEARISH

3. A LOW YIELD, UNDER 2.8% ON THE S & P 500 IS A BEAR MARKET SIGNAL

4. MONEY SUPPLY USUALLY TOPS AND BOTTOMS BEFORE STOCK PRICES

5. THE ANNUALIZED RATE OF CHANGE OF THE MONTHLY SHORT POSITION IS THE BEST SINGLE LONG TERM INDEX I AM AWARE OF

6. MUTUAL FUNDS' CASH POSITION FORECASTS MAJOR MARKET MOVES

7. THE ADVANCE DECLINE LINE USUALLY TOPS OUT BEFORE THE DOW JONES INDUSTRIALS

8. MEMBERS OF THE NEW YORK STOCK EXCHANGE DO VERY LITTLE SHORTING AT MAJOR BOTTOMS

9. THE FOUR WEEK SUM OF SECONDARIES IS USUALLY UNDER 5 AT MAJOR BOTTOMS

10. THERE IS A 37 YEAR MASTER CYCLICAL PATTERN TO THE MARKET

CHAPTER 8

HOW TO COMBINE MARKET TIMING AND STOCK SELECTION

HOW TO COMBINE MARKET TIMING AND STOCK SELECTION

I hope you have breezed through the preceding chapters and now have a general working understanding of the market place. Those of you that have been in this game for a while will have little difficulty grasping my comments on market timing and the various indicators. Newcomers . . . take heart . . . learning the market and the indices is just a matter of time and familiarizing yourself with some new concepts.

DOCTORS HAVE STETHESCOPES

Have you ever thought about that? Doctors have certain tools they use to perform their jobs better. Writers have typewriters. Salesmen have closing arguments and leading questions. Artists have paint brushes, musicians instruments.

How about stock specialists? They too must have tools and these tools are the various indicators we use. The best ones, the ones I've spent a fortune acquiring are right here in this book. Please keep in mind they are tools and as such take getting used to and, as with any mechanical device, will need repair work from time to time. But above all remember that they are tools and you must have tools if you are to speculate.

THE SECRET TO TIMING PROFITS

If you are to succeed in the market you must develop the knack of buying the right stocks at the right time. This is a two dimensional problem. You must face, and conquer both dimensions. Several years ago there was a popular song whose words were "you can't have love without marriage, you can't have a horse without a carriage, you can't have one without the other." That's the way it is with stock market profits. You are going to find profits few and far between if you have market timing but not stock selection. They are even fewer and farther between if you have stock selection but not market timing.

The importance of this was illustrated in a survey done by the University of Chicago in 1966 that showed most stocks follow the market most often. Other university studies have repeatedly shown that stocks, as a general rule, tend to duplicate the average performance and patterns.

A WORD ABOUT YOUR EMOTIONS

Emotions are a funny thing, especially in the stock market. The word speculate comes from the Latin word specular. Specular means to observe. That's fine and dandy but my observations of speculators, and I've seen them all over the world, is that they act on emotions 90% of the time and observations 10% of the time. I know, I do it myself!

You are emotionally hung up in investment decisions for a variety of reasons. The largest, usually, is the money involved. Then comes your personal decision. You have decided to buy or sell a stock and you're going to hate like hell to admit that big brave you made a mistake. It hurts as much, if not more than the dollar loss. Thus, mistakes grow and grow and grow.

By the same token, when emotions are begging you to buy or sell you can pretty well be assured that it's time to do just the opposite of what your emotions are pleading with you to do. The stock market is set up and operated to separate you from your money. It does this in a nice, logical pattern. It works on principles opposite those that govern virtually every other activity you participate in.

As an example, you toss a ball into the air, soon it starts to fall and your reasoning process tell you it's going to fall lower. It does. But . . . just when your reasoning processes tell you it's going to fall lower, it bounces up.

How about relations with people? Someone tells you they like you, they have trust and confidence in you. You make decisions based on this fact and the relationship is good. But with a stock . . . the stock tells you it likes your thinking . . . it moves up. Thus, you judge it will move up more, and what happens? You know, it declines.

When you are happy with profits in the market you should sell. When prices look so bad your broker doesn't even call, you've got to be buying even though your emotions are going to be running scared.

HOW TO TELL WHEN THE TIME IS RIGHT

This may seem like a smart remark to you but I sincerely believe that the way to tell when it is time to buy or sell is to check the list of prerequisites I have given in this book for the short, intermediate or long term investment. When the indices start giving their red or green light it is time to take action.

82

Review what I've given you . . . have the criteria been met? Where's the trading index, what are the breath and volume figures doing. Check your tools or instruments and see what they are doing. The indications you are looking for again are:

SHORT TERM BUY SIGNALS

1. THE MARKET HAS REGISTERED OVERSOLD READINGS

2. THE MOMENTUM MEASURES HAVE BEGUN TURNING UP

SHORT TERM SELL SIGNALS

1. THE MARKET HAS REGISTERED AN OVERBOUGHT READING

2. THE MOMENTUM INDICES HAVE TURNED DOWN

INTERMEDIATE TERM BUY SIGNALS

1. "WILL GO" IS FORECASTING A MARKET BOTTOM IN THIS GENERAL TIME PERIOD

2. THE TRADING INDEX HAS REACHED THE BUYING AREA AT 130 OR MORE

INTERMEDIATE TERM SELL SIGNALS

1. "WILL GO" IS FORECASTING A MARKET TOP IN THIS TIME PERIOD

2. THE TRADING INDEX HAS REACHED THE SELLING AREA AND IS FALLING

3. SPECIALIST SHORT SELLING SHOULD BE HIGH AND BEARISH

As a general rule of thumb, I would advise you to be quick to turn bullish — slow to turn bearish. Bottoms are formed almost in an instant while tops take a week or two to form as stocks are distributed. This is an important point that must not be overlooked.

Once the intermediate or short term indices have moved close to the area for action — the buy or sell zones — you should start looking for stocks to get into. In chapter 9 I'll tell you what stocks you should be following. Somewhere among this stable of stocks you will suddenly notice two or three starting to send out strong vibrations that they are buy or sell candidates.

You will notice these indications by studying the stocks' A/D line as well as its price pattern in relation to the market's price action. Carefully scrutinize the select stocks that are the strongest and apply the criteria already given to you to choose the very strongest in this group.

ALL THAT'S LEFT TO DO

Buy the stock . . . that's all that's left to do! Sounds easy but in practice it can be quite hard. I'll deal with the various problems later in the book. But for now, let's concentrate on what must be the single largest mistake all market participants make when buying stocks. They buy too high or too low.

HOW TO AVOID BUYING TO HIGH OR LOW

Once all your criteria have been met for buying or selling action, you should then wait for a very strong market day . . . strong in the direction exactly opposite the direction you are forecasting for that market. If you think prices are going lower, you must force yourself to wait for a strong up-day when all stocks are up. That's the day you sell or sell short.

If you are waiting to buy, and all criteria have been met, you wait for a hard down day . . . one where the DJIA is clipped for 7-10 points. That's your final signal to get in . . . while the market is down and buy the stocks under accumulation. If you wait for confirmation from the market that you are right in your forecast of a move, you will end up buying at the top of a short term correction and — more than likely be shaken out of the stock or, at best, have a few restless nights.

Buy on down days . . . sell on up days. That is some of the most important advice I can give anyone about the stock market. If you are buying on up days, you are just a damn fool 80% of the time. I know — I'm still tempted to buy on up days and it invariably costs me money or time. I don't like that.

MY PERSONAL CHECK-LIST

Before I make any transaction in listed stock, I carefully and slowly review the following check list to see if all criteria are met. If they are not, I then realize I am taking on a high risk trade. High risk trades usually cost me money. I suggest you buy stocks that fit the check-list 100% if you want to maximize your results.

There is also a tendancy to use the check-list a few times and then become enamored with your success. The reason the stock went up is, you think, your good looks or brilliance in calling market turns. So — you forget to use the check-list and you're right back where you started — with losses.

Playing the market is a business . . . you must avail yourself of all business tools and the check-list is one of them. It is simple, it is repetitive of what I've already said, but it is profitable. If you don't use it, don't blame me for your losses. I want no part of that. This check-list has taken me a long time to develop, quite a bit of money and some rather deep conversations with John Barleycorn.

MASTER CHECK-LIST FOR MAKING STOCK MARKET TRADES

1. IS THIS A SHORT TERM MOVE OR LONG TERM? This dictates which indices to follow.

2. IS THE MARKET READY FOR ACTION? Have the buying or selling criteria been met?

3. AM I SELECTING A STOCK BASED ON ITS ACCUMULATION PATTERN? Leave your emotions behind!

4. DOES THE STOCK ALSO SHOW ACCUMULATION IN THE DAILY A/D LINE? Watch out if it doesn't.

5. HAVE I SELECTED THIS STOCK BECAUSE ITS ACCUMULATION PATTERN AND LINE IS STRONGER THAN ALL THE OTHER STOCKS I FOLLOW? Select the best stock.

    IF ALL CRITERIA ON THE CHECK-LIST HAVE BEEN MET, IT IS TIME FOR YOU TO CALL YOUR BROKER. UNTIL THEN, STAY OFF THAT PHONE AND SIT ON YOUR HANDS. IT'S MUCH CHEAPER.

HOW TO DEVELOP PATIENCE — OR — MY LOSS IS YOUR GAIN

Last week I lost about $3,000 in the market. It was a stupid error . . . I did not follow the check-list. That's stupid, and it's unforgiveable. The $3,000 doesn't bother me nearly as much as the fact I could not sit on my hands. I got greedy, just had to get in there for some action . . . and I sure got it.

Think of that a $3,000 loss.

The same thing can happen to you unless and until you learn my loss is really your gain. I lost money for a stupid reason. I did something I shouldn't have, and I'm the guy that developed the system that has truthfully worked miracles. Think what can happen to you. Unless you play the market with care, you will do the same thing I just did, or worse. Learn from my error.

That's the best way I can get you to exercise patience. Think of the potential damage that can be done, financially and psychologically, if you start jumping the gun and trying to improve upon an already proven system.

HOW TO AVOID WAITING TOO LONG

Waiting too long is a problem very few people have. Most all of us jump into the thick of things too soon. This is true of life as well as the market. We are all motivated more quickly by emotions than by logic.

But, if you find that you are consistently getting into the market too late, I would suggest you carefully review your thinking processes. Are you waiting for confirmation — a market rally — before you buy and a market decline before you sell? If so, you are being sucked into the market by the pros. Don't let them do this to you. Use the rules I've given you . . . they are very good. When they give their signals, take action . . . don't wait until a ten point gain in the DJIA tells you the indices are correct again!

Another possibility for waiting too long might be that you are listening too much to your broker, or still a little hesitant to try my method. If that's the case, I'd suggest you make only paper trades until you see how profitable my system is. By doing that you will build the confidence required . . . the nerves of steel and stomach of iron . . . needed to act at the right time.

You may also want to consider this lesson I learned from a specialist on the NYSE. The gentleman told me that he, as a specialist, liked to reward people that helped him. In other words, when the public was dumping all their stock on him, he appreciated the buyers that would come into the market to help him stabilize prices. He would reward these sturdy souls by quickly taking prices back to where they were.

Think about that for a moment. When the specialist is being inundated with stock, on the buy or sell side, he's going to be forced to reward those floor traders and others who help him take down the stock. He can only reward them by moving prices back to a more favorable level.

Ask yourself what the specialist is most likely to be doing — can you help him? Do, and you'll be rewarded.

THE TWO THINGS I WAIT FOR

There are many things I wait for before I take action, but the primary points I check are the accumulation and distribution rules. Then I wait for the market to get ready by becoming oversold and then giving me a strong down day to act on.

It sounds so simple, just sitting here writing about it, but the practicalities of the market place make it very difficult to follow these almost childish rules. When I make an emotional decision that's wrong, and most are, I reflect upon a morning in 1962 when the market broke badly during the May crash. At the time, I was in college and had just gone down for breakfast at the fraternity house. The morning papers' headlines were ablaze with news of the gargantuan drop and massive losses. As unknowledgeable, unattached, unemotional college students, we all said we'd be buying if we had any money.

Later, throughout my market research, I learned that the majority of the public were heavy sellers on balance the day that the market crashed and bottomed . . . beginning a four year Bull market!

Incredible! By being un-involved, we had been able to buy, on paper, at the right time. Never forget the story about being so close to the trees that you can't see the forest. Wait for all factual criteria given here to be met. Then take your action. If your decision does not meet the check-list standards, wait until it does.

CHAPTER 9

HOW TO KNOW WHEN IT'S TIME TO SELL

HOW TO KNOW WHEN IT'S TIME TO SELL

When should I sell? That's about the most perplexing question a speculator can ask. Seldom does he get any selling advice from his brokerage firm. And, human emotions being what they are, seldom do we, as individuals, want to sell. Instead, we tend to be optimists, always willing to give the stock one more time to recoup our losses or advance just a few more points.

That's why I think this chapter is vitally important. You must learn to spot selling points in the market and on stocks if you are really to enjoy speculating.

The very act of selling can be a bit painful in terms of the emotions involved. I know many people that have ridden their longterm holdings down to unbelievable depths because they didn't want to "part company", or acknowledge their poor investment decision. Anything that causes any sort of emotional pain, in or out of the market, is hard for us to do. Selling either acknowledges an error or puts us out of what has been a good deal. Both are discomforting.

THIS SCREAMS SELL

I get very worried about my stocks when I see that they are undergoing heavy distributions and the intermediate term indices are suggesting the market is in the area of an intermediate term top.

Until both of these things transpire you don't need to worry too much about the market. But when the stocks start showing distinct signs of distribution, the specialists become heavy short sellers, and "Will Go" forecasts a top, etc., you had better listen because the tools of our trade are screaming that it is time to sell.

Don't worry if the tools will be wrong. You can always get back in. There are plenty of cable cars in San Francisco. A new one comes along about every fifteen minutes — ditto the stock market!

It's Friday! Friday has been the strongest market day since the late **1800's**. In fact, Fridays are up days about 65% of the time. That's a fantastic figure, especially when you consider that the next market day, Monday, has the poorest record of any day for posting gains.

This is a real natural . . . Fridays are most often up days, and Mondays most often down days. If you are concerned about a stock and the market is at all questionable, sell it on Friday because the chances are very strong that it will be even lower on Monday.

I have used this technique time and time again . . . especially for short selling. It just so happens that I love to sell short, it doesn't bother me a bit as it does some people. I almost always try to confine my shorting to late Friday afternoons when prices have rallied and there are plenty of upticks to allow me to establish my short positions.

Let's also not forget that the day before any market holiday tends to be up. About 70% of the time the market day immediately prior to a holiday is an up day.

The same "Friday tactic" works here. These two little known facts are most helpful . . . as you can see from the Associated Press news story about the "surprising" pre-labor day rally of 1972. This facet of the market is little known and seldom understood. There are other similar relationships about which you should know.

Monterey Peninsula Herald Saturday, Sept. 2, 1972. **15**

Tradition Sunk By A Low-Volume Rise

NEW YORK (AP) — Wall Street folklore has it that little happens in the stock market the week before Labor Day. But the stock market punched holes in that tradition this past week, with a volatile, low-volume rise.

The market started off with two days of declines, then cranked itself up in an advance that saw the Dow Jones aver-

"We had pre-holiday volume but not pre-holiday price action," said Robert Stovall of Reynolds Securities. "This development was very encouraging, particularly since it came in the face of increases in the prime rate at the major banks."

The higher prime rates were the main factor cited by analysts for the 4.66-point drop

---

They are discussed fully in Art Merrill's invaluable book, "The Behavior of Prices on Wall Street." This book is a must for all market participants.

Along the same line, Yale Hirsch publishes "The Stock Traders' Almanac" each year and it too is chock full of vital information about what the seasonal tendencies of the market are... monthly tendencies, election year tendencies, etc. This too, is a real gem. It can be ordered from the publisher of this book, or The Hirsch Organization, Inc. 6 Deer Trail, Old Tappan, NJ 07675, for $20.00.

The wise speculator will study these repetitive market phenomena and use the strong days or weeks for selling. Additionally, he will note how his stock performs on what should be strong days. If they perform well, fine. If not, something is amiss and the A/D line figures had better be studied quite closely.

A close study of the A/D work will often give you advance warning of when the stock is running into selling pressures. Then it is just a matter of getting out of the stock and waiting for another opportunity to present itself.

It is important to keep telling yourself that the so-called experts in the market, the brokerage firms' advisors and related media will seldom, if ever, tell you when it's time to sell. That is not the most profitable aspect of their business. You must learn to know when to sell and then have the fortitude to do it all by yourself.

HOW TO AVOID SELLING TOO LATE OR TOO EARLY

When publishing my advisory service I found it was very important to learn to let profits ride. I could do this by using stop points and then gradually raising my stop point as the stock advanced. I wasn't worried about selling to take a profit. I was more worried about keeping the stop point below the price so that it gave a margin of protection, allowing me to trail along on the upswing. In this fashion, I found I could overcome the problem of selling too soon.

The trailing stop point works quite well. Its one drawback is that if touched, it means you will never have gotten top dollar. But top dollar is pretty darned hard to come by with any technique. Also, if the stop is close enough, you're not going to lose out on very much of the ultimate rally.

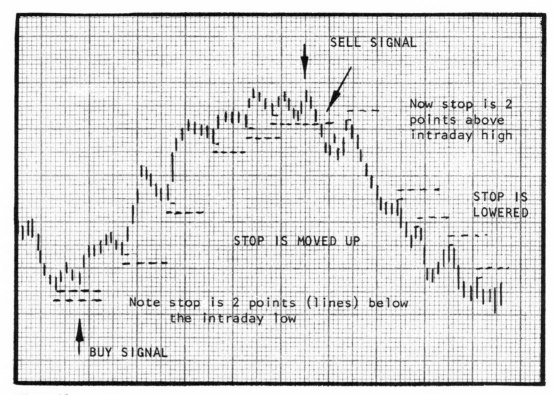

Chart 42

The chart shows how the trailing stop is used. Notice as the stock goes up, the stop is raised. Finally, the stock reacts down to the stop point and the profit is taken. We did not hit the absolute high, but we did manage to ride out some pretty hefty corrections.

This is done by using a stop point that is exactly two points under the stock's most recent bottom area. As a new bottom area is established, the stop is raised to this point. The stop is never lowered and is always kept two points below the most recent base area. This should not be a mental stop. Mental stops don't work. You must give the stop order to your broker to make certain you do not get caught by surprise. That can happen in the market, you know!

A weekly review of the A/D pattern and A/D line will also help keep you on top of the situation making certain that you do not bail out too early or stay aboard too long.

CHAPTER 10

HOW TO BEGIN USING MY METHOD

HOW TO BEGIN USING MY METHODS

Up to this point you have learned the very basics of the method that has been so kind to me. It is now time to learn how to organize these parts into a cohesive and profitable investment approach. After that is done and you have an understanding of my total approach, it will be time to share with you some more market and stock secrets I have learned.

START BY DOING THIS —

The very first thing you must do if you are to be a success in the market is to dedicate some of your time each day to watching and listening to the tools of the trade. You must take time to run some of the figures and then make certain you have time to reflect upon them for a minute or two. If you go at the market in a haphazard way, working at it one week but not the next, in an on-again, off-again basis, your bank account is going to suffer.

Speculating is a difficult job and it requires dedication and a certain amount of time to maintain the vital instruments to hear the market's heartbeat. Thus, you must first decide, and I mean really decide, that this is something you want to do. Once you've made that decision, you will have no problem finding the time to do the work that is involved.

Once you've "given your life" so to speak to speculating, it's time to start working up the various indices I have discussed. This means you will need to purchase a ring binder notebook and rule it off as shown below to keep track of the daily stock market figures. As you can see, all the information you need fits on one page. These records are easy to maintain and will aid in your short and intermediate term decisions.

OPEN	HIGH	LOW	CLOSE	VOLUME	NET A/D VOLUME	CUMMULATIVE VOLUME FIGURE

You'll also need to construct a section for the longer term indices, those whose raw data you will collect on a weekly basis. One page should be devoted exclusively to getting and computing the information for Will Go. That section should appear as follows:

92

BOND/STOCK SPREAD THIS WEEK	SPREAD 5 WEEKS AGO	+/− CHANGE	CUMULATIVE "WILL GO"

Your third and final section for stock market timing tools will contain spaces for the long term timing tools. This page should also be marked off in columns and look something like this:

(WEEKLY DATA)

PRICE AVERAGE	ADVANCING DECLINING STOCKS	MONTHLY SHORT POS.	SPECIALISTS SHORTING	# OF SECONDARIES	MUTUAL FUND ACTIVITY

You will also need to set up some work sheets for following the individual stocks. Earlier in the book you were given the format you can use for setting up these work sheets. One call a day to your broker will give you all the daily stock and market figures you need. Some people (are you listening, Dad) have a hang-up about calling their broker to get figures. They think it will interrupt the broker's busy time. Well . . . usually brokers are not all that busy and even if they are, a good broker is never too busy to give his valuable clients any sort of information. You pay your broker a lot of money in commission dollars. Do not feel timid about using his services. His services are tremendously expensive so get your money's worth.

You'll also need chart paper to plot the various indices. I'd suggest you visit your local blue-print or architectural supply house and get some K & E chart paper. It's green and a bit difficult to use compared to the light blue I use, but it's the best thing readily available. Those of you who want the exact type of chart paper I use can order it from this book's publisher for $5.00 per 100 sheets (minimum order) of 11 x 17 inch paper. This is really the ideal charting paper. I had it especially constructed and printed for my work.

It will take you about five market days to get all your tools assembled but then it's just a matter of keeping the figures up to date on a daily basis and that's not very hard.

WHERE TO GET THE INFORMATION YOU NEED

If you are a newcomer to the market, I'd suggest you turn your attention to a few other good market books that I'm listing here. These are the cream of the crop. Even if you've been in the market for many years, but have not read these books, you should. They are part of the cornerstone of my success:

How To Triple Your Money Every Year With Stock Index Futures by George Angell
Stock Market Trading Systems by Gerald Appel and Fred Hitschler
A Master Plan For Winning in Wall Street by Gene Brady
Technical Analysis of Stock Trends by Edwards and Magee
Profits in the Stock Market by H. M. Gartley
Granville's New Strategy of Daily Stock Market Timing
    For Maximum Profits by Joseph Granville
The Moving Balance System—A New Technique for
    Stock & Option Trading by Humphrey Lloyd
Options As a Strategic Investment by Lawrence McMillan
Technical Analysis Explained by Martin Pring
How I Find Stocks That Double In A Year by Michael Scott
How I Made $1,000,000 Trading Commodities Last Year by Larry Williams

All these books are available from
Windsor Books, P. O. Box 280,
Brightwaters, N.Y. 11718

You'll also want to subscribe to Barron's Financial Weekly magazine and may want to subscribe to the Wall Street Journal. It isn't necessary. You can get the same figures from your broker and when you do need back issues he, or your local library, has all you'll ever need.

As a matter of fact, the Wall Street Journal may be about the worst thing you can subscribe to. I believe this or many reasons. First of all, it is written so well that it grabs your attention and before you know it you can't tear yourself away from one or two stories . . . all of which take time to read . . . too much time for the busy man.

Secondly, if you subscribe to the Journal, you will undoubtedly read the gossip columns on the back page. These supposedly learned columns on the market's activity are, in fact, just gossip and tout columns. Watch out these columns are not only time consuming but will do little to help you learn anything at all about the market. They are full of misconceptions and false ideas. Steer clear of them.

Advisory services can be a big help to you if you will just let them. As a former advisory service publisher, I think I know the area pretty well. I also know just about all of the market letter writers in this country on a personal basis. By and large, they are a good group of people . . . they are doing their best to help subscribers. It's just that some don't have all the skills they'd like. But . . . there are several letters that do openly discuss their indices and will give you additional insight into the market, stocks and the entire scope of trading strategies. These letters can be very educational and informative. You will want them for their educational value, not their advisory value. Try you best to learn their tricks of the trade. Some of the better services that do share their knowledge with subscribers are:

- **COMMODITY TIMING**
- **COMPARATIVE MARKET INDICATORS**
- **DEMARK FUTURES FORECAST**
- **ELLIOTT WAVE THEORIST**
- **INSTITUTE FOR ECONOMETRIC RESEARCH**
- **PROFESSIONAL TAPE READER**
- **PROFESSIONAL TIMING**
- **SYSTEMS AND FORECASTS**
- **ZWEIG FORECAST**

WHO WILL HELP YOU?

There are two basic groups of people who will help you in the market — those who are brokers with good experience and those who have advisory services. Individual brokers and the smaller, one man services will really provide you with more information, suggestions and help in constructing indices than anyone else I know.

HOW TO USE BROKERS TO YOUR ADVANTAGE

I've already mentioned the need to establish good rapport with your broker and to make certain you freely use his services for quotes, etc. There are other functions he can perform. One is providing you with research reports from his firm's research department on the various companies you are following.

I have found one particularly good firm, Goldman Sachs, and my broker there knows what stocks I follow. If he hears or sees any important news he's in touch with me right away to tell me of the latest developments.

Again, remember that most all brokerage firms have libraries of investment books, the Wall Street Journal, etc. Use these services. You pay for them every time you give your representative an order.

But let me caution you not to use brokers for very many of your investment decisions. After all . . . you have my million dollar Accumulation/Distribution system and believe me, it will outperform any brokerage firm recommendation in an up or down market.

That's because it is a realistic approach to the market place based on concrete facts that we can all see and measure. Brokerage firm recommendations, on the other hand, can be dispersed for many reasons. The most common of which is to sell stocks!

Many investors are not aware, but it's true, that on many of the stocks their friendly broker tries to sell them, the brokers are paid an extra comission for the selling. In other words, the broker gets the normal commission plus an extra bonus for selling this particular stock. That's pretty frightening. If someone wants to get rid of a stock so badly that they will pay brokers extra moeny to drum up some pigeons to take down the stock, you know there's little in store for the upside potential of that issue.

To my way of thinking, this is a gross conflict of interest. There should be a law that forces brokers to disclose when they are selling a stock for a premium, how large that premium is and who is paying the premium. But there isn't . . . and probably never will be. The NYSE is a close-knit bunch of people.

HOW TO PAY LESS IN BROKERAGE COMMISSIONS

Commission costs will eat into your capital, if you're not careful. It is vital to shop around to get the best service at the lowest cost possible.

Essentially, there are just two types of commission houses — the full-service firms and the discounters. Among the full-service houses are Merrill Lynch, Prudential Bache, E. F. Hutton, Shearson, and Dean Witter Reynolds.

Stock commissions at these houses are quite high. You're paying for your broker's advice. With these techniques, you won't need it.

There are two ways to cut your commission costs. You could go to a discount house, with substantially lower rates. The largest is the very successful, reputable, Charles

Schwab Discount Brokerage, 101 Montgomery St., San Francisco, CA 94104. I can recommend them highly.

Your other alternative, if you have a good relationship with your current broker and want to stay with him, is to try to negotiate a better price. This is usually most successful if he values your business and is afraid you'll go to a discount broker.

If you're an active trader it would be wise to use one of these approaches. You can imagine what a savings you could realize. Last year alone I transacted over fourteen million dollars worth of stock. At an average of 2%, that's about $280,000 in commissions. Just as in any business, you must watch out for your overhead. In speculation, commissions are your single largest overhead expense.

WHAT STOCKS TO FOLLOW

This next section is almost as important as the chapters on market timing and accumulation and distribution. Study it closely.

Through the years I have devised a method of selecting stocks to follow. It is a four-part method that seeks to identify the type of stocks to follow and then points me in the right direction. The first method is one that selects stocks to follow from the most active list. The next method selects stocks that are good traditional growth issues, while the third method keeps its ears open for special situations and the fourth and final method concentrates on the flyers or stocks that respond well to market moves.

The most active stocks are very difficult to trade. For this reason, I am not a big follower of the most active issues. They are too dominated by the public and the antsypants, mutual fund gun slingers. Nonetheless, there is one important point here you should not overlook. When the market has entered an intermediate, or long term buying area as our indicators say, then check the most active list and see if you can spot any stocks that are making new yearly highs in spite of the crunch in the market.

If so, you have a potential big winner on your hands. The criteria again are a severely oversold market of intermediate or long term consequences and a stock on the most active list (use the weekly twenty most actives published in most all Sunday newspapers) soaring to a new high for the year. Follow such stocks closely. Some of the all-time big winners have been spotted in this relatively simple fashion.

Good long term growth stocks are one of my favorite categories of stocks to follow with the accumulation/distribution figures. Selecting such vehicles is really pretty easy. In fact, one can do it with just a set of long term chart books. There are also some standard long term growth stocks that I like to follow and suspect will be around for a long time to come. They are McDonald Corp., Polaroid, Burroughs, Walt Disney, Rubbermaid, Clorox, MGIC Investment Corp., Atlantic Richfield, Tandy Corp and Syntex.

HOW TO SPOT LONG TERM GROWTH STOCKS FROM THE CHARTS

This is a simple matter of just thumbing through a long term chart book that gives stocks' trading activity for the last ten to fifteen years. By doing this you will notice there are a few stocks that just never seem to go down . . . they are in almost straight up trajectories. These are good growth stocks. That's the quickest way I know of locating them. Let a stock's past trading history tell you if it's been a growth stock in terms of the market price. If so, chances are it's worth following for even high prices or an excellent short sale should it finally reach its ultimate high, which I believe the A/D work will indicate most all the time.

Special situations are a difficult thing to locate and follow. Usually, when someone is putting you on to a special situation, you are in the process of being "bagged." Perhaps not intentionally by the party doing the touting, but nonetheless, special situations are usually just that, "special situations."

But, just like, you, I get turned on to these special deals from time to time. I listen intently to the song and dance routine as to why the stock is going to zoom to the moon by next Wednesday. Then, and this is important, I work up the accumulation/distribution figures for the stock to see if the special situation story is really bullish or just real bull! That trusty little line invariably tells me if my information is good.

My favorite trading vehicles are the hot stocks that follow the market . . . the flyers. These, too, are pretty easy to spot. Current stocks I'd label as flyers are Digital Equipment, New Process, Itek, Hilton Hotels, Control Data and similar stocks. *

These are the issues that are most responsive to the whims of the markets. Like commodities, they move in a hurry. What you are looking for here are stocks that top and bottom at the same time as the market. Selecting such stocks isn't difficult at all. Just compare the stock with the market and see if it moves in unison, except with greater magnitude, than the market. If so, you have a potential flyer — a stock well worth following.

*(Ed. Note: These stock recommendations were made in 1972, when the original edition was printed).

A SPECIAL SECRET ABOUT SELECTING STOCKS TO FOLLOW

Some readers of this book are going to be disappointed with the next few paragraphs. That's because I'm going to level with you and tell you to keep away from the low priced $10 to $30 a share stocks. If you were sitting here in my office with me, I'd plead and beg with you to never trade in the low priced issues. I say this for several reasons that I'd like to go over with you.

The most important reason is, to be brutally frank, that my accumulation/distribution work doesn't perform in its usually exemplary fashion with the low priced stocks. In fact, I have a hard and fast rule; I do not follow any stock under $30.00 a share. You shouldn't either. I know this means you will miss out on a few of the early stages with a few of the big winners, but that doesn't matter. What you need is something that is consistent.

Stock priced over $30.00 a share is more consistent and reliable to work with than the cheapies. Why? You see, the low priced stocks are most attractive to people who have less money . . . to the raw boned pennyspeculators who have no idea of what they are doing. They swing from hot to cold in a matter of minutes. This results in wild and choppy trading patterns for the stock . . . and this pattern, so wild and erratic due to the emotioanl cross currents of the small traders, is most difficult to follow.

Stay away from the low priced issues!

Not only are they dominated by the public, but most maniuplated stocks are in the $10.00 to $25.00 a share category. These are the stocks some promoter runs up, sells to the public and then the S.E.C. stops trading. The promoter is out and the public is holding the bag. Once a stock has broken above the $30.00 area it loses its emotional public following and picks up professional traders, people like myself, who are more objective. The stock then develops a much better trading style . . . one that is infinitely more trendable and predictable.

WHEN TO MAKE YOUR FIRST TRADE

Don't begin making any decisions with real money until you have   first charted the A/D work on a stock to cover the two most recent market turning points. There can be no set time period, but this usually means you need about two month's trading action before you start to see what is really taking place in the A/D figures. It is necessary to compare the stock with the market and the longer time period you have with which to compare, the better an idea you will have of the accumulation.

99

After the above has been done, it is almost time to make your trade. You are following the market figures and are in receipt of market action signals to buy or sell.

Then it's a question of ferreting out the best candidates. Personlly, I like to put my money in the three best stocks. I'd do this even if it meant that I had to use Odd Lot orders. There is comfort in diversification and sometimes the second or third of the three best stocks will really catch fire and be the big winner.

So . . . make your selections and then carefully review the check-list one more time. Have all the criteria been met? If not, why are you planning to take action. You certainly did not learn from my loss.

THE FIVE MOST COMMON CAUSES OF STOCK MARKET LOSSES

Besides not following my check-list, there are five other common causes of loss that I want you to be well aware of, so you do not go out and start making losses right off the bat. From time to time you should review this list to see if you are not making some of these common errors. It's pretty easy to slip into any of these money-wasting devices.

1) PLUNGING — This is perhaps my greatest market sin. I think nothing of putting every single cent I own into the market and then going on margin. It's great when you are right, but when you're wrong . . . it really hurts. This has happened to me one time and I hope never again. There is no need to try to be a market plunger. Plunging only shortens the amount of time needed to make you lose your money. Be content to trade with most, but not all, of your funds.

2) SOPHISTICATION — It's amazing how market newcomers end up getting into up and out, lower case Monogolian reverse straddles, strips or other very sophisticated investment tools. They try to arbitrage between the Pacific Coast Exchange and the Big Board, etc. These are all highly developed tactics that even the biggest boys in Wall Street have trouble with. We should only concern ourselves with buying and selling and selling short. Beyond that, we are getting too sophisticated for our own good.

3) DEMANDING THE EXACT HIGH AND LOW—Why we all insist on getting the exact high or low of a move I'll never know. But we do. In our efforts to do the seemingly impossible, we end up getting confused, bewildered and removed from our money.

When you start playing the market that closely, you experience all sorts of frustration and emotions. I say this despite the fact I have frequently gotten the exact low of a move. Seldom, though, have I hit the exact high. When you go gunning for the impossible you start bucking too many probabilities and losing control of your emotional calm. When that happens you'd better go take a cold shower because you are not going to be making any smart investment decisions.

4) LETTING LOSSES RIDE —   As soon as your trade shows a loss it screams out that the investment decision was most likely wrong. Should this decision be proven wrong three days in a row, it is time to admit the error and quickly move. You cannot wish a stock back up. You cannot influence the price of a stock so you must react to what it is doing. If it is going against you, admit that fact and close the trade.

Too many people try to wish their stock back up a few points so they can bail out at a break-even point. Seldom does that happen. I know of one gentleman who bought 1,000 shares of a stock at 65 . . . it was his life savings . . . and stubbornly refused to admit he had made an investment decision that was wrong. At 62 he should have gotten out but didn't . . . he kept waiting for the stock to go back to 65.

He's still waiting for the stock, now at $4.00 a share, to go back to $65.00 . . . a very sad story!

5) EMOTIONS — I've already harped on this enough, but it's impossible to stress too often the need to maintain your cool and refrain from going off on emotional binges. It is so easy when you are making money like crazy — thousands of dollars each and every hour the market is open . . . maybe five to ten thousand dollars in just a matter of days. Such binges, if dominated by emotions, can end up giving you some pretty large monetary hangovers because you get out too soon.

In the art of speculation you are going to be your worst enemy. Never forget that.

CHAPTER 11

HOW TO START MAKING MONEY IN THE MARKET . . . TOMORROW MORNING

HOW TO START MAKING MONEY IN THE MARKET . . .
TOMORROW MORNING

When I first thought of writing a book, I contacted one of the major publishers in this country. They were enthused, but wanted the book written in a certain style and slanted to make my method seem like the perfect panancea to all stock market problems. To top it off, they repeatedly told me a summary chapter would not appeal to readers.

Maybe it doesn't. I don't know, but I would not feel right without trying to meld the elements together for you. A thumbnail sketch of what I hope you have learned in this book is as follows:

1. Set your personal goals
2. Determine what market trend you are going to follow
3. Select stocks to follow
4. Work up the A/D line for the stocks
5. Work up the market timing tools
6. Wait for a market buying or selling point
7. Take action only when the check list conditions have been met

Setting goals and determining what trend of the market one should follow is a personal decision. There's not much more I can add. It is something that every man should choose for himself based upon his own emotions, time and money.

STOCKS TO FOLLOW

It is best to keep your money involved with the more volatile, more active issues. These are the ones that spurt 10 to 20 points in a week's time. They will usually be high priced stocks, but that's just what you want. Don't fool around with the low priced cat and dog issues.

The following list of stocks should be a good group to follow over the coming years. Undoubtedly, you will want to add and subtract from this list, but it's a good basic list from which to begin. These stocks are also quite responsive to the A/D approach as well as cyclical patterns.

Notice that I have given the cyclical pattern for all stocks. The distance or time span indicates the amount of time usually seen from one bottom to the next in these issues. The astute student will notice there are varying time periods and will make notations on his charts when the next bottom is expected to occur based on the time cycle given here. Do not be afraid to change the time periods. I'm certain several of these stocks will move into slightly different trading patterns over the next few years.

STOCK	SYMBOL	BOTTOM TO BOTTOM COUNT
BAUSCH & LOMB	BOL	8 WEEKS
BURROUGHS	BGH	7 WEEKS
CONTROL DATA	CDA	7 WEEKS
CURTISS WRIGHT	CW	10 WEEKS
DISNEY	DIS	4.5 WEEKS
ITEK	ITK	5.6 WEEKS
MCDONALDS	MCD	14 WEEKS
MGIC INVESTMENTS	MGI	12-13 WEEKS
NATOMAS	NOM	8-9 WEEKS & 18 WEEKS
POLAROID	PRD	4.5 WEEKS
SYNTEX	SYN	13 WEEKS
WINNEBAGO	WGO	6 WEEKS

KNOW WHAT THE PROS ARE DOING

After acquiring the back data, notebooks, chart paper and other tools of the trade, it is time to begin carefully following the techniques discussed in the first part of this book to detect professioanl accumulation and distribution. Do not overlook these vital aspects of stock selection. Both selection techniques are paramount to making profits. Carefully compare your stock to the market, then focus on the A/D line to see what the pros are doing.

Are they buyers or sellers? That's the question you must answer.

If they are buyers, it will not be profitable to buck their forces. They have considerably more capital and information than you do. Frequently a trader gets an idea "fixed" in his mind that a stock will go up or down. It's his pet stock. This is fine, but when you start arguing against the accumulation figures and dictating what the stock is going to do, you will run into lots and lots of trouble.

The market, or individual stocks, don't give two hoots for what you think is going to happen. We cannot influence prices, we can only notice what is happening and key off the signals. You will be able to see what the pros are doing by:

1. CHECKING FOR THE ACCUMULATION OR DISTRIBUTION PRICE PATTERN
2. COMPARING PRICES TO THE A/D LINE
3. CONFIRMING THE ABOVE WITH CYCLICAL BEHAVIOR

HOW TO RATE YOUR TRADES

To facilitate selecting your stocks you may want to use the matrix given below to screen out the best stocks. There are three columns. I leaf through the pages of my chart book and check off what, if any, columns the individual stocks qualify for.

STOCK	BUY/SELL PATTERN	A/D LINE BUY OR SELL	TIME CYCLES SAY GO?

You can run through 40 to 50 stocks in about 10 minutes this way. If you follow only 7 to 15 issues, which is what I'd suggest for beginners, it takes even less time.

After going through your list of stocks you will notice that very few have qualified on all three counts. That's the way it should be and those few are the stocks you should try to take positions in. The strongest stocks will be the ones that get a check in all three columns.

If you have more than 2 stocks meeting all qualifications, I'd suggest you turn your attention to the A/D line to see what stock has the strongest price, volume relation and then "bank" on that one.

It is not necessary to follow jillions of stocks. I think the most common error traders make is they try to chart or follow far too many issues. You will find all the opportunities (and trouble) you'll ever be able to handle in 10 actively traded flyers. There is no need for the average person to follow many more. When I published my advisory service, I only followed 40 stocks on a daily basis. Now that I'm not publishing I only follow 15 and I've given you 12 of them!

WHAT TO DO WITH YOUR PROFITS

At first glance the above comment seems a bit strange . . . we all know what to do with our profits. Or do we?

I have two rules for market profits. The first is to let your profits ride as long as possible. That's not exactly earth shattering, but it is important to learn to hold onto the stocks with the profits and sell the ones with losses.

For the moment, imagine yourself as a retail merchant selling sweaters. You have ordered two different styles for this year's business. You promote both and suddenly find you are sold out of sweater "A", while sweater "B" has barely moved.

Would you call your supplier and order more "B" sweaters? Hardly. You would order more of the A variety.

If you think this analogy doesn't apply to the market, you'd better rethink your concept of profits and losses. Speculating is a business. Any intelligent businessman gets rid of his dogs while concentrating on his hottest items. The stock market is no different.

Another lesson we can learn from studying successful businesses is to see what they do with their profits. Do they siphon them out of the business through high salaries, etc.? Of course not. Profits are retained for expansion, research, etc.

I try to handle my investments in the same manner. The majority of my profits are kept in the market to increase the total business operation I have in trading or investing. It's the old adage of reinvested profits and the mathematics of what happens with reinvested gains is phenomenal.

As an example, if you start in the market with $1,000 and make $500 on your first trade you then have $1,500 to work with.

Let's say your next trade sees a 20% gain. If you were wise and reinvested your profits, your net gain would be $300. A spendthrift would withdraw the $500 saying he could do it again. On his 20% gain he would then make only $200.

I'm not advocating that you be a miser and hoard all market profits, but I do encourage you to retain the bulk of your earnings . . . especially as you get started . . . so that you can begin pyramiding your way to wealth.

MY FINAL COMMENTS

I sincerely wish you a profitable career in trading stocks. I firmly believe it can be accomplished once you have digested this book. If you will but take the time to understand what is in this book, then begin applying the information, you will quickly see many buying and selling opportunities. You will be able to time your purchases in conjunction with market rallies while limiting your sales to the beginning of market declines.

I suggest — in fact I strongly recommend — that you trade for the intermediate term trend of the market. It is much easier and the profit opportunities can be immense compared to the nominal risk taken at the extreme oversold conditions we see throughout the year.

I also want to make certain you understand the necessity for using stop points to limit your losses. If you do not use the 3 point must system, you are just a damned fool. You must use stops. If you don't you are going to have some losers get away. Then you'll blame me, your broker, the stars or whatever when the blame really belongs to the person who did not use the stop point. The two methods given here are wonderful, avail yourself of them.

Above all, keep your eyes peeled for those super strong accumulation line signals . . . the immediate profit signals. They are great little indications that an immediate move is starting . . . and will give you almost instant profits.

I can't stress enough the importance of following the accumulation/distribution figures. They are such powerful indices of a stock's strength and are the real backbone of my success. I'm certain you, too, will be able to use them to spot stocks that will skyrocket just as I have. I hope you will be able to pick the next Bausch & Lomb at 50 and sell it at 150, then short it at 190 and ride it down to 60 (adjusted for the split) as I did.

Or perhaps you will have the good fortune of loading up on several thousand shares of a stock in advance of some special news break that sends prices up 5 or 10 points in two days. It is one of the world's most exhilarating feelings. It can happen to you if you will apply my methods in a consistent manner.

There'll be losses, but if you follow my system your losses will never be more than three points while your gains can be unlimited. You now know how to handle losses and profits, how to detect accumulation and distribution, how to forecast market action. The final step, that of learning to regulate and control your emotions, is something you alone must work on. Start by doing the opposite — that's right — the exact oppostie of what they are telling you to do.

Once your emotional conflicts are resolved, you will be on your way to the most rewarding life style I have ever seen. You can really be your own boss subject only to the pressures to which you want to submit. Your wealth will be dependent upon how much time you want to put into the market.

May I personally wish you good luck and good trading.

CHAPTER 12

PRICELESS TRADING HINTS

PRICELESS TRADING HINTS

Up to this point I've been trying to give a unified program for operating in the market. Now it's time to give you some of the gems of wisdom and tactical procedures I've learned along the way.

Hopefully, this chapter will give you some added insight into the market as well as improve your strategy to further refine your timing and selection.

HOW TO GET THE BEST EXECUTIONS

The secret of getting the best executions lies in selecting the very best stock broker and brokerage firm. This means you need a firm that has efficient communication systems and a broker who does exactly what you tell him and places your orders exactly as you instruct.

Another facet of getting the best possible executions involves playing the "players", in other words, trying to outguess the rest of the herd. Let's see how this is done.

WHEN TO BUY AT THE OPENING

For the most part, people who buy at the opening are not showing very good judgment. The opening price is usually highly artificial and established at the whims of the specialists. There are only two times when I want to buy stocks on the opening.

The main reason to buy at the opening will be to take advantage of a special news or market situation. As an example, the market has been in a vicious selling wave and closes sharply lower on Monday. You might then wish to use opening orders for Tuesday's market on the assumption that prices will be briefly dumped on Tuesday, then spin around and establish a new uptrend. In that case, buying onto expected weakness, it is permissible to buy on the opening.

The only other time I want you buying on the opening is when the indices tell us prices are headed substantially higher and the technical climate is one of continued bullishness.

An example here would be when short term buy signals have just been given and prices have faltered for a day or two continuing their basing pattern.

Late one afternoon a vigorous rally comes in closing up an otherwise down market and giving bullish trading ratio readings. It is then safe to buy at the opening the next morning on the assumption that the short term trend, which was bullish, then had a correction and is once more ready to make a run. This method really acknowledges that it would have been better to buy on the previous day's close, but since you couldn't make that, the next best shot will come bright and early the next morning.

WHEN TO USE MARKET ORDERS

Many authors suggest you always use market orders. I don't. I think they are very dangerous and quite costly. My account has proven this to me time and time again.

When you get so all fired wrapped up in a situation that you must use a market order it simply says your emotions are in complete control. They dominate your every move and that's not the way it should be.

I use market orders only for buying into selling climaxes or selling into buying climaxes.

This means I must see the market off 10 to 15 points after an already "too long" decline. Then, and only then, I consider using market orders as I toss them in while prices are still off for the day. Once the trend has reversed those using market orders will find themselves paying the high for the day.

Signposts that it is all right to use market buy orders will be a negative tick figure of −700 or more, a trading index reading of 2.50 or more, 180 or fewer unchanged stocks for the day, a 20 point loss two days in a row for the DJIA. The point here is that market orders should be used when the market has entered an extreme overbought or sold area.

WHEN NOT TO BUY ON THE OPENING

Buying on the opening can be very dangerous . . . it should almost never be done. This is especially true if the DJIA were up 7 points or more the previous day. A move of that magnitude usually means there will be a short term pull back and opening prices will be close to the highs for the day.

Any time you use market buy or opening orders after the DJIA has been up 7 points or more, you should have your head examined. It's just not a safe way to place your orders.

HOW TO USE STOPS AND WHERE TO PLACE THEM

In my opinion you should use stop loss points on every single trade you ever make. I don't care if it's a short, intermediate or long term trade. You should use stop points. I cannot emphasize this enough. I only wish I were a more persuasive writer so that I could conjure up a few words that would stick in your mind forever . . . words that would force or intimidate you into using stops with all your trades.

There are two ways to arrive at stop points. The first is my own "invention", the second, a product of W.D. Gann back in the 1920's.

Mr. Gann's method is the simplist, thus the best for beginners. The method says that you place a stop loss order 3 points above a short or 3 points below a long. That's all there is to it. It doesn't make any difference if the stock is selling for $15 or $150. Your stop point should be three points below your cost. The only changes I make here is that on stocks selling for more than $90 I recommend the use of a stop point 5% below your cost.

Do not let the simplicity of this method fool you. In fact, its simplicity is its greatest advantage. You never need to be in the dark about where to put your stop.

It's automatic . . . if you must trade you must use stops. Thus, I call this the three point must system. It will always keep you safe from sizeable losses and you will seldom be "gunned" for by the specialists.

Should you switch to a bit more sophisticated manner in your use of stop points, I suggest you use my personal method. This method is based on playing the players. It is done by carefully examining a chart of your stock and then deciding where the other longs, or shorts, have most likely placed their stop points.

Then place your stop point just beyond theirs.

Chart 43

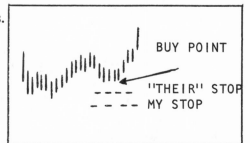

110

My thought on this method rings along these lines: If the specialists are going to gun for stops, they will most likely get into, but not beyond, the majority of the stop points. Additionally, if I am to be stopped out I want to make certain they get everyone else as well. This type of stop point gives me the psychological advantage of feeling slightly better when I am stopped out because I know all the other people were stopped out before me!

Super short term trades may also want to consider the use of a time stop point. All other methods for stop points have been based on price. That is, a stock must move X%, X points, X distance above a margin average or trend line, etc. to produce a stop point.

That's fine and dandy, but my work shows we can also use time stop points. These you must keep track of yourself and work like this. You buy a stock expecting it to move from 40 to 50 in 10 days. If the stock has not begun its move within 4 trading days, close out the position.

In other words, if the stock cannot get going and do what our work indicates it should something is wrong and let's get out while the time is still good. If a stock can't start performing within 4 days, the chances are slim that it will suddenly catch fire. This time stop systems can be used only with stocks selected by my million dollar accumulation distribution formula. That's because signals given by this system demand immediate market action. If such action does not follow, let's step aside.

A WORD ABOUT MENTAL STOPS

I'm always asked if one should use mental or actual stops. My answer is that you should use actual stops. Mental stops are not accurate, are seldom used and subject you to too much of an emotional strain. With every buy or sell order you give your broker, you should also give an actual physical stop point. He must follow that for you.

I don't know one single person that has the emotional stability and nerves of steel to successfully use mental stops. I say this despite the fact I know hundreds of professional traders. Mental stops are almost impossible to use.

HOW TO FORECAST DAY TO DAY ACTION

Forecasting day to day market action is the simplist of all forecasting if one is aware of the basic day to day pattern of market activity. The basic pattern is that all market days see three waves of activity.

111

An up day will see an up wave, down wave and then renewed upwave. A down day sees the reverse with a down move, pullback rally and final down move. It's my estimate that these three wave patterns account for 85% of all daily trading trading activity.

Thus, if you suspect an up day tomorrow you can be 85% accurate in assuming it will open up, rally for two to three hours, sell off for two hours and surge ahead at the close. A down day forecast just reverses this action.

You can forecast an up day for tomorrow if the DJIA is off for the day, but there are more advancing stocks than declining stocks and the DJ utility average was up for the day.

I also look for an up day when the market has been down, but 6 or more of the 10 most active stocks were up for the day.

Perhaps the most important ingredient in forecasting the next day's market action is to note what took place in the last 45 minutes of trading in today's market. If the market closed strong, expect that rally to continue or "spill over" into tomorrow's market . . . even if there's a weekend in between.

Conversely, when the market closes weak, especially after being strong for most of the trading session, you can bank on the next day's market to extend the weakness. The last hour of trading is a real must for you to follow if you decide to trade the market on a shorter term basis.

Other suggestions of what will happen in tomorrow's market today can be gleaned from taking note of where the market is in reference to the Yin Yang cycle. Are prices in the oversold area? If so, the chances of a rally are increased. When our indices say prices are in the overbought area the probability of declines will be enhanced.

You should also be aware of how many days the market has been moving up or down. Once its streak of up or down days is 10 or more days, all in the same direction, expect reversal action.

HOW TO CAPITALIZE ON THE THREE HOUR CYCLE

Time and time again I've noticed myself and other traders, or investors, trying to establish positions paying high prices over the short term because we fell prey to what I've identified as a vicious three hour cycle.

The cycle is unique in that it seems to force us to do the wrong thing at the wrong time on a pretty consistent basis.

Usually something like this happens: We decide it's time to buy and have located a stock under aggressive accumulation. Our next step is to make the actual purchase.

Being intelligent speculators, we wait for a strong down day . . . the trap is about closed. But . . . before we place the actual order we are frightened and decide to wait until there's some strength coming into the market to validate our upward forecast.

So, we wait. Sure enough prices start to rally.

Then we realize that we were right and try to buy, but only on our terms, below the current market. Prices continue moving up, ditto our buy orders. Unfortunately, the buy orders are not filled.

This action continues for exactly three hours. Then we can no longer take it . . . we throw in market orders and buy our stocks at the high of the day just as the current three hour cycle ends and a new down move begins.

As I've seen this pattern repeated time and time again, it was interesting to me to discover that psychologists have noticed a similar pattern in human behavior.

In one test done at Northwestern University, groups of college students were exposed to speakers with views dramatically different than the groups. Little persuasive change was made at the end of one hours exposure and even less change at the end of two hours exposure. The most sizeable reversal of student's opinions occurred after three hours of exposure to the ideas that were presented.

Similar studies have shown subjects become extremely restless after three hours of boredom. In fact, boredom has been shown to follow a bell shaped curve wherein the first hour without external stimuli produces little boredom, the second hour more boredom with the third hour seeing the greatest boredom and restlessness peak, cresting as this emotion withers away.

These studies simply confirm what you can see every day in the market. Short term moves last about three hours which is just long enough to convince our emotions that we'd better get back into the game. That, of course, is exactly the wrong time to take action.

Only experienced traders can resist this emotional three hour jag or those who realize just how vicious this pattern can be.

Keep in mind that our three hour cycle works on the down side as well as the upside. In fact, just about all forms of market action have mirror images reflecting the other side of the market.

On the downside, the three hours occur when you want to short or sell a stock and gets you to follow the stock down, on weakness, before you sell to the professionals who then act contra emotions, take your stock at the start of a short term rally!

The next time you are about to make a purchase or sale, stop to see if prices have been moving in your forecast direction for the last three hours. If so, wait and take your action later unless you like to buy high and sell low.